Anthony Esolen

Reflections on the Christian Life

How Our Story
Is God's Story

SOPHIA INSTITUTE PRESS
Manchester, New Hampshire

Sophia Institute Press
Box 5284, Manchester, NH 03108
1-800-888-9344

www.SophiaInstitute.com

Sophia Institute Press® is a registered trademark of Sophia Institute.

Library of Congress Cataloging-in-Publication Data
Esolen, Anthony M.
    Reflections on the Christian life : how our story is God's story /
Anthony Esolen.
        p. cm.
    ISBN 978-1-933184-85-2 (pbk. : alk. paper) 1. Christian life. 2.
Storytelling—Religious aspects—Christianity. I. Title.
    BV4501.3.E845 2013
    248.4—dc23

                                            2012037395

£4.50
ge

18|46 .

Reflections on the Christian Life

To my wife, Debra, and
my children, Jessica and David

Contents

Foreword

This book is an attempt to meditate upon the meaning of a Christian life insofar as it is a story, and as the story of the life of Jesus sheds light upon it. My qualifications to write such a work seem paltry enough. I'm not a saint, I have had no private revelations, and I do not teach theology. If the reader wishes to enter most deeply into the life of the God-Man who walked the hills of Palestine twenty centuries ago, I should recommend Karl Adam's *The Lord*, Edward Leen's *In the Likeness of Christ*, G. K. Chesterton's *Everlasting Man*, and François Mauriac's exquisite *Life of Christ*. All I can bring forth in my defense is my teaching of literature. I have spent many years introducing students to the works of the masters, Homer and Virgil, Aeschylus and Sophocles, Virgil and Ovid, Saint Paul and Augustine, Boethius and Aquinas, Dante and Chaucer, Shakespeare and Cervantes, Herbert and Milton, and many more. So I have had to think a great deal about what it means to live in a world of stories, and what makes the Christian narrative so distinct, fulfilling all that is true in the others, and surpassing them.

If I should say anything here that in any way strikes the reader as inconsistent with the plain meaning of the word of God, or with the teachings of the Church, or even with the advice and insights bequeathed to us by the saints, I beg him to forget what I say and forgive me my error. I don't wish to commit the sin of originality. But if these words can point one soul in the way toward the true Author and Judge of all, they will have done their modest work.

Reflections on the Christian Life

Chapter 1

At the Shores of Eternity

Some years ago a young man, intelligent and lonely, found himself in a European airport with a day and night to wait for his flight back to America. He was hungry and had no money. Then an older man sat beside him and engaged him in conversation. The older man saw that the lad had nothing to eat, so he offered him his ham sandwich. The man was a Catholic priest.

That young fellow, as it turned out, had never been baptized, but he was on a search for truth—for what it means to be a good and fulfilled human being. He did not forget the priest's act of kindness. A few weeks later, at the school where he was enrolled as a first-year graduate student, he attended a pulled-pork party thronged with fifty or sixty other English students and professors. Some of them were cheerfully indulging in a favorite pastime, singing old Appalachian hymns in shape-note harmony. That was when he tossed out the opinion that Saint Paul was a bigot, because of what he said about women not being chosen for the ordained ministry. A young Roman Catholic heard him, put down his plate, and took up the challenge to set him right.

What happened after that, I'll wait to tell. First I want to make an observation about time; for we can't appreciate fully what it means to live in a world of stories, unless we see what it means for God to be the Lord of time.

When Saint Augustine was a young pagan struggling to understand the truth about God, he had first to clear away his fleshly notion of what it meant that God should be everywhere. He thought, as the old Stoics did, that God was present throughout the universe, like air or light that fills a room, with more of God being in a big thing, such as the earth, and less of God being in a little thing, such as a grain of sand. He didn't see then that he had demoted God to the status of a creature, if even the greatest creature imaginable. It took him years—he says this with honest embarrassment—to conceive of just what God meant when He said to Moses, "I AM." If God is the One Who Is, He cannot be divided into parts, or bounded by boundaries, or parceled out into more and less. That means not only that God is everywhere. It means that the fullness of God is everywhere, God in His infinity. G. K. Chesterton put it marvelously in a lyric poem. The speaker asks the wise men of the world whether they know what is in "the smallest of the seeds." Scientists can't say, and philosophers can't say, but the believer sings out in wonder:

> God Almighty, and with Him
> Cherubim and seraphim,
> Filling all eternity,
> Adonai Elohim.

That's something the secularists of our time can't or won't understand. When a Richard Dawkins, the rather silly atheist zoologist, conceives of God, he imagines some big creature tinkering with the laws of the universe at the onset of the big bang, turning knobs and pressing buttons so as to fine-tune everything to result in the world we know, the world with blue jays and mockingbirds, dogs and cats, puffy clouds in the sky, and grass beneath our feet. Then he says that it is absurd to suppose that such a creature exists. Well, it is absurd, because that imaginary *creature* is not God. First, God is not just big. He is infinite and omnipotent. It is easier for God to create a universe billions of light-years in its vastness than it is for me to add seven and three — infinitely easier, for "easy" and "difficult" do not apply to God. That is one of the things the sacred author meant when he was inspired to write, "And God said, 'Let there be light,' and there was light" (Gen. 1:3). Just like that; He spoke, and it came into being.

But second, God is not next to or outside of His world. He is present in His fullness everywhere. So it is not a matter of fine-tuning from a distance. In the wisp of a dandelion seed, what is there but God, all of Him, and the hosts of heaven singing His praises? In the dash of a photon along an optical fiber, what is there but God, all of Him, in His infinite act? He is not simply great because He comprehends the greatest of things. He is great also because He is comprehended by the smallest of things; and that too is a measure of His love.

Now what is true of God and objects in space is true also of God and objects in time. The Deists of the eighteenth century got themselves tangled up in error because they had a childish view of God. They often thought of Him as a creator, a kind of clock maker, who existed "before" the universe, who then fashioned this vast machine, and then let it run by itself. If they had read Augustine, they would have learned that there is no "before" and "after" with God, because it is God who created time to begin with. Just as God is present in His fullness in the most far-flung galaxy and in the tiniest of particles — for the whole universe is as nothing to Him—so He is present in His eternity in the most fleeting of moments, just as in the billions of years since the world burst into being. That is what Scripture means when we read, "One day is with the Lord as a thousand years, and a thousand years as one day" (2 Peter 3:8).

But what does that mean to us? What does it mean to the stories of our lives?

Recall the words of the prophet Isaiah. The Jews had fallen away from true worship of the Lord. They had forgotten Him. So God speaks to His forgetful people, "Can a woman forget her sucking child, that she should not have compassion on the son of her womb? yea, they may forget, but I will not forget thee" (Isa. 49:15).

We forget things, because we dwell in time. When the face of a friend is far away, it becomes a bit hazy to us; when the years pass by, it becomes hazier still. But that is not God. He is here, fully, and now, fully. He can no more forget us because of the passage of time than He can miss us because of the distance of space. And He will not forget us, nor will He abandon us; so we can say with the confidence of the Psalmist, that even if we should descend to the nether world, yet He is there.

That means that now, here, is the meeting place of time and eternity. Now is the acceptable time, and, as Jesus says, "the kingdom of heaven is at hand" (Matt. 10:7).

Let us place ourselves in imagination in a humble dwelling place in Palestine, two thousand years ago. A young maiden is within. Perhaps she is preparing bread for the day. Perhaps she is sitting and meditating upon the word of God. All at once she is met by a messenger of the Lord. We do not know what she sees. We do know the words that are spoken to her, words that break like a battering ram through the walls of a ruined world.

At the Shores of Eternity

All of the history of the Jews, and indeed of mankind itself, has been looking forward to this moment. All of the future of man's salvation will look back upon this moment. This is the breach in man's hard heart, this is the hinge, this is the flinging wide of heaven's gates. And Mary said, "Behold the handmaid of the Lord; be it unto me according to thy word" (Luke 1:38). And the Word was made flesh, and dwelt among us.

We Catholics believe that that was the moment of the Incarnation, when the world changed forever. We are right to believe so. But is that all? Is it a moment done and gone? How can it be, when God, the Father, the Son, and the Holy Spirit, is present in His eternity here and now? When we worship Jesus in the most holy Sacrament of the Altar, we are not merely setting up a memorial to Him. That is what we do for heroes of old, who live and do their great deeds and who pass away. But Jesus Himself is the Way, the Truth, and the Life. He was and is and always shall be the Eternal Word of God. So our memorial is other than a memorial, as the bread is other than bread. When did Jesus sacrifice Himself for us? Two thousand years ago, on a dark Friday, atop the Place of the Skull. And now, and always, and in a most intimate way in the Sacrifice of the Mass.

Or come with me to a quiet road on a sunlit afternoon. Two men are walking to the nearby village if Emmaus. They have been witnesses to dreadful events they do not understand. Their teacher, whom they honored as the promised savior of their people, has been brutally put to death by their overlords, at the instigation of the chief priests. All their hopes have been dashed, but then, strangely enough, some women of their company now say they have seen Him alive, and sure enough, His tomb is empty. They don't know what to make of it. But a stranger falls in with the two men on their way, and He engages them in conversation. He interprets the Scripture for them, showing them that it had been foretold that the Son of Man would be put to death by wicked men, but then rise again on the third day.

Their hearts burn within them, but they still do not recognize their new acquaintance. When they reach the village at evening, they beg the stranger to tarry with them awhile. He does. They enter an inn, and when they sit down to eat, the stranger breaks the bread and blesses it. Instantly are their eyes opened, and they see Jesus, who then vanishes from their sight. They recognized him, says Saint Luke, in the breaking of the bread (Luke 24:35).

Isn't this moment, too, in its own way, the moment in which all things are made new? Until Jesus broke the bread, the disciples were lost in sorrow and confusion. Nothing in all the tumultuous events of the last few days, or even in the many preceding centuries of God's covenant with Israel, made sense to them. It was not a story, but a jumble. Then He broke the bread, and opened their eyes. They could see that it was Jesus with them.

So with the eyes of faith we too see that Jesus has not passed us by. He did not continue along that road long ago, abandoning us to our confusion. He tarries with us. The inn is now the Church, and we see Him and adore Him who breaks the bread and who is Himself the broken bread. And when we partake of that bread, we join not only the disciples at Emmaus, but the saints who have gone before us and the saints to come, those feastful friends of the Bridegroom, who rejoice in the supper of the Lamb.

The point is that, just as God dwells in His fullness here in your private study, here in the walk by the river, here in the little schoolroom, here in the hearty family celebration, here in the holy joining of bride and groom, here in the quiet chamber of death, so too every moment is the turning point, every moment the acceptable time, every moment the moment when we are to hear His voice. This is the moment, now, as you read these words, when all things may change, and like the young son in the parable you will say, "I will arise and go to my father" (Luke 15:18).

So the story is not something with a faraway beginning, leading to a faraway end. It is the story that does not end, because it is always beginning again, among us here and now.

Then the young Catholic defended the honor of Saint Paul, in the midst of people who believed and those who did not believe. He said that Paul had turned the world upside down. For from now on it would mean nothing to have been born a Greek or a Jew, a freeman or a slave. Nothing, that is, in comparison with Baptism. For that is the moment upon which everything in our lives depends. When we die, now, it is not the passing away of our bodily functions that we are talking about. We die to our old selves in Baptism. We drown those old selves in grace. We die with the crucified Christ and then live with the risen Christ. Then, members of one body, we look upon one another and say, "My brother in the Lord!" That is to look upon bigotry as from an infinite height and instead to love the gifts that God has bestowed upon one's brother or sister.

The young questioner thought about that. He did not shrug it away. As the weeks went on, he continued to ask questions. He remembered the priest in the airport and decided he would look into the nearby Catholic church. He began to attend Mass once in a while. He and his Catholic interlocutor became friends. Then, after about a year, he said to his friend, "I've decided. I am going to be baptized." So in a church filled to capacity, on the Easter Vigil, in 1984, he and his friend, and many others too, approached the altar of God, he to receive the sacraments, his friend to be the spiritual sponsor. The new Catholic, the new Christian, never lost his faith as time went on, even though he lived and worked among the secularists of an American university. He eventually married a Catholic woman, and they have adopted children, whom they are happily raising in the Faith.

What did you see, Mary, on that morning long ago? "I saw the tomb of Jesus who had arisen, and bright angels attending." It is not long ago. It is now. It has never ceased to happen. We do not say, "He was risen," but "He *is* risen." And the next person you meet, in an airport, at a picnic, or walking down the dusty lane to Emmaus, is just that person for whom the whole history of the world has been preparing. There can be no greater adventure than ours.

Chapter 2

The First Good News

When my first child was born, my daughter, Jessica, she fit within the crook of my arm. I held her and fed her from a bottle, and smiled at her, and chattered, and looked at her eyes, which seemed to come from another world. So my wife said, and I believe she was right.

Yes, I know that the skeptics will laugh at me. The skeptics, those so poor they do not even know how poor they are, we will always have with us. When I say "another world," I don't mean that our little baby existed somewhere, waiting patiently for a body to dwell in. I mean that she was new. She came to us from outside ourselves. My wife and I were not her ultimate beginning. The first good news for all of us, the first joyful story of our lives, is that there is a story at all, and an Author who has loved us into being.

Hear the proclamation by the beloved John: "In the beginning was the Word, and the Word was with God, and the Word was God" (John 1:1). The words we speak, says Saint Augustine, have a beginning, a middle, and an end. In fact, we can say a word only if we allow the sounds we make to pass away. But that, he says, is not so with God. The eternal Word spoken by the Father is the Son, who was with the Father "in the beginning." We mustn't think of that as some first moment in a string of moments, the first domino to fall in a chain of dominoes. What John means is that at the heart of everything, before there were the heavens and the earth, and now during the time wherein we changing creatures dwell, and after these heavens and this earth shall be no more, stands the Word, through whom all things are made. The Word is not only *in* the beginning. The Word *is* the beginning and ever will be.

Several centuries before Jesus was born, the wise men of Greece asked the question, "What is the *arche* — the beginning, or the foundation — of the world?" They did not ask what was *their own* beginning, and that was probably their greatest mistake. Some of them said that air was the beginning, meaning that at the basis of all things is that ever-changing air. Others said it was water, because we see that water can take the forms of solid, liquid, and vapor. Still others said it was both air and water, and fire and earth to boot, combining to constitute mud or iron or flesh or whatnot. Some of a more mathematical bent, noting the beautiful harmony inherent in natural things, said that it was number — and indeed the Jewish writer of the book of Wisdom would say that God created the world "in weight, measure, and number" (Wisd. 11:20). The Stoics said that it was something they called *logos,* or "word," the intelligible and everlasting order of the world.

But there is something funny about all these suggested beginnings, and that is that they don't really *begin*. They are attempts to explain what underlies everything we see about us, but there is no sense that the whole world, from its foundation to its consummation, is a story with a beginning that is ever beginning anew, and an end, the kingdom of God. And that end, where is it but also present in the beginning and, as Jesus says, even now at hand, at the very gates (cf. Mark 13:29)? So when Saint John reveals to us, "In the beginning was the Word," he is not at all saying that the Greeks had it right. He is correcting them, we might say—if we keep in mind that his correction blows their world sky high, as high as God and His heaven! For the Word we are talking about here is not static. Nor is it something pronounced and then done. The Word is Christ, the wisdom of God. When the Lord speaks, says the prophet Isaiah, his Word does not depart from Him in vain. The Word makes things happen; it is a two-edged sword; its Spirit is a mighty wind upon the waters, making them bear fruit; it enters the heart of the believer; it parted the seas for the Israelites and fed them bread *from* heaven; it immerses the Christian in living waters and gives him the bread *of heaven.*

So we Christians believe, really, in a beginning, and not just something or other that happened first in time. A beginning actually begins something. Think now of the things that begin and of the holiness of their coming to be. A good Christian man and woman pledge their lives to one another. I see a photograph of my own father and mother, impossibly young and radiant, he in a white suit and black tie, she in a wide flowing white gown, holding a bouquet of flowers. They were, as is just and right for young people, ardent in their love. My father was a good man and a devout Catholic, but he had been tempted to preempt the beginning of their married life. He is now with God, I trust, and will not blame me for telling the story. My mother gently refused him, and for that act of purity and true love he was to thank her forever after, and he told her how glad he was that when he was weak, she was strong. They waited until the true beginning, and the Word of God, Christ Himself, was with them.

They settled down to live in rented rooms, just around the corner from the church. They couldn't afford a house in those days, not even to rent. And there, in the privacy of the night, by the grace of God, the two became three. They became a family, although it would be a little while yet before they became aware of it. We read in Genesis that the Spirit of God was brooding upon the waters, when God said, "Let there be light," and there was light. The wonder of creation, of bringing light out of darkness, of *beginning,* is renewed again with all holiness when the Christian man and woman, made one in Christ, bring into being a living soul. For each little child is like a church, bigger on the inside than on the outside—more vast than all the rest of the universe, and timeless. The universe is seeded in time, but the child is oriented toward the time beyond time. The universe is bounded by what is, but the child is oriented toward what is to be. Every time a child is conceived in the holy embrace of marriage, it is the Word that speaks sacramentally again, and we can cry out with the psalmist, saying, "Thou sendest forth thy spirit, they are created: and thou renewest the face of the earth" (cf. Ps. 104:30). And I was born and christened after my father, Anthony, from whom I had in part my beginning in the flesh, and made my small entrance into the Church, both the one just around the corner, and that never-failing one founded by Jesus and to be brought to its joyous consummation.

How many, indeed, are the things that begin! In holiness only do they begin; otherwise they merely start up for a while and then fade. Many centuries ago, a youth named Anthony wandered into a church in Egypt and heard the gospel about how Jesus spoke to the rich young man with love and said, fairly pleading with the lad, "One thing thou lackest: go thy way, sell whatsoever thou hast, and give it to the poor, and thou shalt have treasure in heaven: and come, take up the cross, and follow me" (Mark 10:21). Do we see the invitation? Jesus does not paint for the young man a fable of flowery fields and easy conversation at the riverside. It is a *cross* that he will have to carry, but it is *Jesus* whom he will follow. If he takes up the offer, he will be as naked as a babe entering a new world. But the gospel says "he was sad at that saying, and went away grieved: for he had great possessions" (Mark 10:22). He saw only the darkness of the door and did not enter.

But others did. On that day in Egypt a saint was born. For Anthony took the good news to heart. He sold his inheritance and gave the proceeds to the poor. Then he began to live for God above all, advancing like a brave young soldier into the desert to pray and to do battle with the enemy, and many they were and are who would follow in his traces. When Francis, dressed in all his finery, rode past the leper with the festering sores and, against the promptings of his fallen nature, returned to him to kiss his mutilated hands, a saint was born. For Francis took the good news to heart and began to live for God above all, gathering about him a veritable army of fellow soldiers and friends, and teaching Christian hearts to be children again, singing for grateful joy, for the beauty of creation, and the infinitely greater beauty of Jesus.

Then by all that is holy, let them begin — let us return again and again to those words of power, "In the beginning was the Word, and the Word was with God, and the Word was God." Not so long before Jesus was to give Himself to be slain by wicked men — that is to say, by us — only a few days before His Passion, the followers of Jesus, His good friends who hardly understood a word He said, were squabbling over who would be greatest in the Kingdom. They were bound to time, and they thought in time. They thought that the Kingdom would come to be, in the same sense that the Roman Empire had come to be, only that the Lord's kingdom would not fail. They had in mind the wrong sort of kingdom, and the wrong sort of beginning. So Jesus took a little child and set him in their midst. And he said, "Whosoever shall receive one of such children in my name, receiveth me: and whosoever shall receive me, receiveth not me, but him that sent me" (Mark 9:37). What did he mean by that? Surely that it is only by humbling ourselves, by emptying ourselves of all our supposed importance, that we can be filled with God. Yet I think now that perhaps the child also stands as a reminder of those quiet and momentous beginnings, when something new enters the world.

For the child's life is full of beginnings. He comes to be. He leaps in his mother's womb. He is born, is separated from his mother, and opens his eyes. He sees the eyes and the face of his first love in the flesh. He is baptized with water and the Spirit and anointed with holy oil. He hears his name and does not know it. He hears his name and does know. He takes his first toddling step. He speaks a word. He opens the word of God — I opened it, in the days before I have any clear memory, and read, "In the beginning God created the heavens and the earth" (Gen. 1:1).

We are then to be like that newborn, or like the child in the strong hands of Jesus, who heard those words of beginning, and who shall suppose that the child did not take them to heart, just as Anthony and Francis did? When did God say, "Let there be light"? He said it in the beginning that was, and he says it in the beginning that is now. When was the Word with God? In the beginning, before the light of the universe, and now, before the light that enlightens the heart of man. He says to us, "Come with me, and I will make you live."

Recall the old miser in the Christmas story that we all know and do not understand. In the house of his poorly paid clerk, he hears one of the sons reading to his brothers and sisters from a book: "And he took a small child, and set him in their midst." Their brother, the little crippled boy, is gone, but remains a fount of blessing for them all, even in their grief. Then the heart of old Scrooge begins to break—or begins to beat; it amounts to the same thing. He will repent. He will keep in his heart the feast of the littleness of Christ.

When he awakes that morning and finds to his joy and surprise that it is Christmas Day after all, he hardly knows what to make of it. "I don't know anything at all," he cries. "I am quite a baby!" Indeed he is. So was I, for a few moments of special grace, when I looked into the eyes of my daughter and knew for the first time that I was something new in the world, a father. So must we all pray to be. Little children sit on a parent's lap and sing out in their small voices, "Tell the story again!" Just so, God, the eternally young, spangled the heavens with stars and peoples the world with creatures greater than the stars, with little children. "Tell the story again," they say, and they mean, "Let it all begin again! Go back to the beginning!" And our Lord Himself, who desires that we should be like little children, tells us over and over, "Let there be light again! Turn back, turn to the beginning!"

Well may He do this, and well may He Himself be the light from darkness that enlightens every man. For the Word was made flesh, and dwelt among us, and we beheld His glory, glory as of the only-begotten Son of the Father (cf. John 1:14).

Chapter 3

A Journey to the Lord

The young woman in the faraway province of Britain had heard many tales of the wonders and the riches of the empire, in part from her teachers, but mainly from other women, the wives of legates and proconsuls and generals and such important men. The tales might have roused envy in a woman of frailer character, but not in Helena. She cast a bemused eye upon them, as upon fine brocaded gowns that seemed stale or overdone, or that simply did not fit her figure. So too did she hear the fables of religious enthusiasts and philosophers. "Put your trust in Mithras, and he will save you!" they cried, but she would hesitate and ask, "Who is this Mithras, and why should I trust him?" And they could give no answer.

Then one day she spoke with a learned man named Lactantius, a Christian. "What is different about your Christ, whom you worship?" she asked.

The reply was straightforward and stunning. "Well," said Lactantius, "he walked the earth in the flesh, and performed miracles, and was put to death by the Roman authorities in collusion with the priests and scribes of the Jews, and rose again on the third day. This all happened during the reign of Tiberius Caesar."

"How do you know that he rose?"

"His disciples saw him and spoke to him. Five hundred at once, in fact. Then they wrote down what he had spoken to them and what he had done."

This is beginning to be interesting, Helena thought.

Such is how the novelist Evelyn Waugh imagined the conversion of the commonsensical Saint Helena, mother of the emperor Constantine. Helena had little interest in the city of Rome or its politics, but instead embarked on a pilgrimage to the Holy Land, to unearth from its ruins the true Cross, at the site where Jesus had been put to death.

She was hardly the first pilgrim. We know from eyewitness testimony that many Christians, from the earliest years of the Church, traveled to Palestine to walk the paths that Jesus walked, and that the Christians who dwelt there could point to a cave and say, "Here was the stable where Jesus was born," or to a rocky outcropping that the emperor Hadrian had tried to bury under a pagan temple and say, "Here was the tomb where Joseph of Arimathea laid His body to rest."

It is a deeply human thing, the desire to return to a place of joy or sorrow or wonder or peace. A few days ago I was riding in the car with my son, through the county in Pennsylvania where I was a boy. I took the meandering way home on purpose, so that we could pass certain places. Here was the cemetery where my grandmother and grandfather were buried, over there, near the edge, on that hill. Here was the house—if you take away the new wing—where my father and his nine brothers and sisters grew up. Here was the nearby playground, which is now no playground but the grounds of a big warehouse, where I used to go when we visited. Here is the church where my father served as an altar boy, in the days when Father O'Neill had hopes that he would become a priest. This is called Sandlot Street, because before we built our house on the land—the house we would always call "the new house"—the boys of the neighborhood played ball there, and so did I.

Or I recall, in my youth, walking into the woods up to a bare knob of rocks and glacial debris, with my old collie at my side, to look out for miles upon my ragged town, with all its abandoned coal mines and heaps of coal refuse lying like patient mountains. There in the winter, with dusk coming on, I would look at the pale blue shadows lying upon the snow and think about the last summer, with the blueberries on the northern side of the hill, and about other years long past, when I was small and first climbed up the escarpment with my father, and about years before that, when my grandfather walked along the coal miners' paths, to gather berries or to hunt for mushrooms, or to cut a corner in crossing to the far side of town.

We are surrounded by so great a cloud of witnesses, cries the writer to the Hebrews (Heb. 12:1), and if that is true of the life of the spirit, so is it also true, in a wistful and bittersweet sense, of the ordinary human life that comes into being and passes away, swift as a weaver's shuttle. In the basement of my mother's house there is a pool table, and a mere glance at it brings me back: suddenly the dank room is bright and warm and dry, and men and boys, my uncles and my cousins, surround the table, chatting, eyeing up the trick shot, each of us holding a secret "pea" with the number of our ball on the table, hoping that it will survive until it is our turn, and then, after sinking other players' balls and collecting dimes from them, sinking our own, worth a quarter from everyone—quarters, and vows of revenge, and laughter. And I can see the glittering eyes of my cousins, who are now far away, and my uncles, who are old and who no longer shoot pool, and my father, who was buried in the cemetery on the hill behind our church, twenty years ago this Valentine's Day.

We do our small part to remember. We take pictures, we erect statues, we tell stories. But without the Lord, it is all like a lean-to hustled up against the wind. When the children of Israel lived in captivity in Babylon, their captors, perhaps with genuine sympathy, perhaps wishing to cause pain, begged them to sing the old songs of Jerusalem. But how, cries the psalmist, can we sing of Jerusalem in a foreign land? "If I do not remember thee, let my tongue cleave to the roof of my mouth; if I prefer not Jerusalem above my chief joy" (Ps. 137:4, 6).

Yet our own powers are not sufficient. We do forget. We cannot help but forget. Here is our "old house," where we moved when I was a toddler, and where my brother and my sisters were born. This is the living room where I took baths in a metal bin for the ashes from our coal furnace, since we had no bathtub then. Here was the window for the coal chute, now boarded over, where I would wriggle inside to open the door when my mother had forgotten her keys. Here is the front stoop where four feet of snow was once piled high for a fortress, with a room inside, big enough then for me. But just as the snow melted away and left not a trace that it had ever existed, so these memories of mine — and memories of your own, my dear reader — will melt away, and leave not a trace.

Or perhaps they will not melt away. Now I am thinking of another pilgrimage, but one that is unique in the history of man. While the Jews were in captivity in Babylon, far from their beloved home, their captors were conquered in turn by the Persians, and the Persian emperor Cyrus, an enlightened despot, gave the Jews permission to return to Palestine and to rebuild the holy Temple. They did so, but the cultural connection between them and the Persians must have endured for a while. For the Persians passed down a tradition that a great King would arise in the west. Like the Babylonians before them, the Persians were avid astrologers, and they connected the birth of this King with the appearance of a special star—or perhaps what we might call a special asterism or planetary conjunction. So, late in the reign of Caesar Augustus, three wise astrologers or "magi" (the word is Persian) followed that heavenly phenomenon to the west, charting its course in the sky against the pattern of the fixed stars, until its motion reached what looks on earth to be a standstill, and they found themselves in the vicinity of Jerusalem.

The rest of that story we know from the Gospel of Matthew. But perhaps it is too familiar to us. When the poet T. S. Eliot imagined it in "The Journey of the Magi," he placed it in the memory of one of the wise men, looking back upon "the hard time we had of it," with the refractory camels, and the crowded inns, and the innkeepers charging high prices, only to come to the home of the newborn King they were seeking, and to know, with a shock, that all their pagan past must be swept aside. It was like witnessing the death of the old gods, says the narrator, who ends the poem with the confession, "I should be happy of another death."

For, whether they understood it fully or not, they were on a pilgrimage to seek something *entirely new*. We go to Gettysburg and say, "Here is where Pickett led his gallant charge, doomed to defeat," but we do not ever go somewhere to say, "Here is where the history of the world will change forever." But that is what the wise men were doing. Even their gifts confess it. They gave the Christchild gold, not because they knew for a fact that he was a king already, but because it had been foretold that

He would be king. They gave the Christchild frankincense, not because they knew for a fact that He was a priest already, but because, whether or not they were aware of it, it had been foretold that He would be the priest of His people. They gave the Christchild myrrh, not because they knew for a fact that He would die for the sins of the world, but because God in His infinitely wise providence had ordained that it should be. They were, we might say, on a journey to memorialize not what had been, but what would come to be.

It was a journey, then, of hope. And here let us also be wise. For God, a day is as a thousand years, and a thousand years as a day; He is not subject to time, but is its creator and Lord. So the events of the life of Jesus are ever before us, in a special way in the Eucharist, but also in our own pilgrimages to the heavenly Jerusalem, the City of Peace. When Saint Helena journeyed to Palestine, she was not seeking a memorial of something great that had passed away, as a military historian might travel to Gettysburg to unearth some bones or some ordnance. She was, in her way, accompanying the wise men on their journey to what is yet to come. That is what all Christians do, and that is what separates us from the common world of men who remember, or forget, and die.

When we hear the words of Jesus at the consecration of the wine, "Do this in remembrance of me," we Catholics do not simply understand it as a bare memorial, like a plaque set up on a bridge or a carved stone set in the wall of a new building. For the Sacrifice of Jesus happened once, on Calvary, but also happens now, not as something repeated, but as something that has burst the limits of time and place, so that we partake of His Sacrifice really and not just in memory, just as we will partake of it eternally in the wedding feast of the Lamb.

A Journey to the Lord

Since that is so, we too may join the magi on their journey. The holy childhood of Jesus is not a memory, not something past and dispensed with, but something new and awaiting our arrival. But attend to what that means for us. Shall it be that we join a tour with the saints and hear the guide say, "This house is where Jesus dwelt as a small boy with Mary and Joseph, and in this room the magi presented Him with their gifts of gold, frankincense, and myrrh"? Not at all. Nothing can be lost from the memory of God, for whom to remember is to see and to see is to foreordain. The house is still with us, and there, in a way we cannot now comprehend, because we are yet corruptible and our minds are dim, dwell Mary and Joseph and the boy Jesus, with Mary weaving a cloth for her husband and Joseph smoothing the leg of a chair with chisel and pumice stone, yet all bright in the light of the risen Christ. It is the heart of the collect for the feast of the Holy Family. We visit that house in Bethlehem, or the later home in Nazareth, and learn from Jesus, Mary, and Joseph the virtues of family life, so that we and our families may be united in the joy of the house of God forever.

So it is not true that the good things we have known we will never see again. All that is lost will be found and trans-formed. John the Evangelist does not reveal to us that we will forget the earth, but that there will be "a new heaven and a new earth" (Rev. 21:1). He reminds us that although we do not yet know what we will be, we will be like Jesus, and "we shall see him as he is" (1 John 3:2). And this Jesus, who walked our earth, as Lactantius said to Helena in the story, and who spoke to people, and broke bread among them, and knew the joy and the heartbreak of friendship—this Jesus, who came to bring us life and that in abundance, will not despise the small and humble memories we cherish, and which he shares with us, in his blessed humanity.

But behold, his star is here, in the heavens. Let us be on our way.

Chapter 4

Fling Wide the Portals

On the fortieth day after Jesus' birth, Mary and Joseph took Him to be presented in the Temple, offering the poor man's sacrifice of a pair of turtledoves, as prescribed by the law of Moses. There they were met by the old man Simeon, who had been waiting to see with his own eyes the salvation of Israel. He took the child in his arms and cried out joyfully, "Lord, now lettest thou thy servant depart in peace, according to thy word: for mine eyes have seen thy salvation" (Luke 2:29-30). Then he prophesied to Mary that the child would become a sign of contradiction for many, that the thoughts of men might be revealed; and that a sword would pierce her heart.

There's a great portrayal of this moment by the Renaissance master Andrea Mantegna. Mary's arm leans partly out of a window toward the viewer, as if we too are meant to be present at the scene, or as if the prophecy applies to us also. Mary is a hardy young woman with a determined and protective look on her face, holding the child tight; Joseph looks on from the background with stern and furrowed brow. And the baby Jesus, wrapped in swaddling clothes now, as in death He would be wrapped in the shroud, is crying. I imagine that while this scene was transpiring, out in the courts and alleys of the city, merchants were hawking their wares, as if there were nothing better in the world to do than to buy and sell, and laborers were sweating under their loads and glancing toward the sun to see how long it would be before they could return home to food and rest, and children were running about and getting into careless trouble, and yet the long-awaited Messiah, Jesus most holy, was there among them, and they knew it not.

We shouldn't blame them too harshly. It is always so with mankind, and especially now, in a secular world. What a poor and sickly thing it is, that secular world, and how flat and tepid and aimless are its stories! I once attended the wedding of two people who had lost all connection with the Lord. They were Jewish, and so they had the requisite rabbi, and the cry of "*Mazel tov!*", and the dance, with the groom's father sitting in a chair and hoisted aloft by four or five men—I was among them—to shouts of good cheer. The look on the man's face was one of complete abandonment to happiness. That couple would be divorced within a year or two, with a prodigious settlement upon the bride, who, as it seems to me now, never did understand anything of love, much less of the ancient faith. "Except the Lord build the house, they labor in vain that build it" (Ps. 127:1).

And except the Lord be the author of our lives, we labor in vain to write them. We scribble our accounts of material success, a prestigious job, a house too big for life, children whom we drive into stardom, cruises and jaunts to exotic places, and in the end it is insipid, and all the noise of it but serves to mask the truth that there is no deep melody, and all the pungency of it but serves briefly to appease our abiding hunger.

Many years ago, I spent a summer at a Catholic Worker house in Washington. There was at the time a notorious advocate for the homeless, running a large shelter near the Capitol. He had abandoned his wife and children to do this, and the result was that he dwelt in constant anger, shut off from spiritual counsel; and the shelter was a den of drugs and crime. The husband and wife who ran our home advised people to stay away from there. They themselves could take only a few guests at a time, both men and women, but they tried always to open their hearts to the guests and—what is the same thing—to lead those guests, little by little, to the heart of the Lord.

There were, in that house, stories of terrible suffering and sin. But John and Polly said morning prayer every day, inviting the guests to join, and when there was a priest available, they prepared a small table for Mass. I remember one old man, on the wagon, who joined us all the time and was skilled in carpentry and plumbing and a host of practical things. He had stories to tell and was far from his home in the Midwest. It seemed for a while that he would join the house permanently and give himself up to the service of God. Then one morning we awoke to find that he had left without a trace. No doubt he was running away from God, but to run away, in that desperate fashion, is far better than to fail utterly even to notice the demanding holiness of the Most High, and so I have hope that the story of that old man did not dwindle away and that God overtook him at last.

So God overtook the young Thomas Merton. He had lived a life of dissipation, an empty secular life, focused on the noise of success, with work that did not satisfy and women he did not love. Then he wandered one day into a city church. It was, we might say, as if his life had been given the dimension of depth, as he was introduced to the holy. He heard the priest at the pulpit giving a sermon on the nature of the Eucharist, and how the Lord Jesus was truly present under the appearances of bread and wine, and there, in the pews, listening to the scholastic theology and apparently understanding it in mind and heart, were common people, housewives, construction workers, janitors, old men and old women, youths and children. And Merton was abashed. It was as if he had walked out of a flat and unreal world, into a fullness where truth dwelt.

When we bring our children to the church to be baptized, what are we doing? If it is only a matter of doing what our parents and grandparents did — only a secularized tradition — then, as far as we ourselves are concerned, it is really pointless. It may even be a kind of dried-up idolatry, like that practiced, perhaps, by a Pontius Pilate. We should not believe that sophisticated Romans in the time of Christ actually believed in the pantheon of the Olympian gods. When Peter denied Jesus and became aware of it, he wept bitterly (Mark 14:72). But the educated Roman, if faced with suffering, would have denied in a trice Jupiter and Juno and all that lofty stable of lecherous gods and goddesses. The religion was subordinated to secular purposes. To solidify their hold on subjugated nations, and to justify the despotism of the empire, the Romans encouraged a cult of *Augustus et Roma*, the worship of the all-devouring city and its emperors. Those worthies, upon their death, would be deified. That explains the last dry witticism of the dying emperor Vespasian: "I believe I am becoming a god."

I am not saying that such baptisms are ineffectual. God does indeed shower grace upon the infant baptized, who genuinely becomes a member of the Church, but *we* are still making a mockery of it unawares. I have been present at such scenes. And I have wanted to cry out to the parents, "Open your eyes; look about you! An entire world, the true and profound world, is waiting for you to enter it." In that world there are the depths of time and the incomprehensible vastness of eternity. The baby is baptized, just as Jesus was baptized by John in the River Jordan. And just as Moses led the people of Israel across the waters of the Red Sea, from slavery in Egypt to the Promised Land, so now Jesus immerses us in His death and Resurrection, and we pass from sin's bondage to a life that makes all our petty concerns as insubstantial as the shadow of a shadow.

When my mother took me to daily Mass as a little boy, so small that I thought the priest's voice was coming mysteriously from the walls, she was introducing me to that world. It was all around me, in word and deed. Paintings of heroes from the Old Testament—David and Solomon, Moses and Aaron, Gideon and Samuel, Isaiah and Jeremiah, Daniel and Ezra, looked down upon me in their mystery—as did the scenes upon the ceiling high above, of Mary crushing the head of a serpent while standing upon the blue globe, and robed men I did not then know—Dominic and Thomas Aquinas—looking on in adoration, while a muscular archangel Michael thrust his sword below. The church was like a great cavern during those daily Masses. I believe, in the silence and the solemnity of the Mass, that I somehow knew that I was entering into a momentous history. Is there any place in the world where one can pass into a new dimension, like a character entering a fuller world, to be woven into its glory? Look at the doors of the church.

So when Mary and Joseph took Jesus to the Temple, we must not judge them as we might judge ourselves. They did not do so because it was the thing to do. We have before us the man whom God had chosen to protect the childhood of His Son, the man whom the Gospels, so chary in their praise, call just and upright, and the sinless Mary, whose heart was plunged into the will of God. For them, it was the dedication of their Son to God, the God who had worked wonders in all the long history of Israel, from Abraham to the present moment. If it makes sense to say so, they were introducing the child Jesus to His own Father, just as later in His young life they would teach Him to read the Scriptures and to say the holy prayers of old. A man might say to his son, "See, here is the picture of my father in his uniform, before he landed at Normandy," and so usher him into the family pieties that extend from age to age. That is a good thing. But how much greater, how much more beautiful, to say to your son, "See, there upon the altar, in the monstrance, is the Lord Himself, who gave Himself up to death on a cross long ago, that our sins might be forgiven, and He still gives Himself to us, and always will."

Jesus said that He had come so that His disciples, and we, "might have life and … have it more abundantly" (John 10:10). When we look upon our fellowmen who do not know the Lord, we should desire also to introduce them to that life, which is life indeed. We have no idea what will happen. It is the Lord who gives the increase.

I remember a young man, very bright but in a narrow way, whose family life had been flattened by divorce and whose mind had been turned by the despisers of religion. He himself did not despise it, and he joined our Christian men's group at the school where I teach, to discuss philosophy and theology. But there was something barring the way. I have no idea what it was. The saints tell us that it is almost always sin, and not some intellectual difficulty, that bars the way. The last I heard, this once-promising young man had given himself over to drugs and was leading a life, if *leading* is the right word to use, that was going around in secular circles, which is to say nowhere.

Yet all it takes is to enter those doors. Or have I got the matter backward? Joseph and Mary entered the doors of the

Fling Wide the Portals

Temple to present Jesus to the priest, but that is because they had already opened the doors of their hearts to God. Listen to the powerful words of the hymn:

> *Fling wide the portals of your heart,*
> *Make it a temple set apart*
> *From earthly use for heaven's employ,*
> *With prayer and praise and love and joy.*

The Holy Spirit desires to dwell within us, and He is the sanctifier, the One at work in all of the history of God's people. When we fling the gates of our hearts wide open, then it is that the Spirit comes to make of us a holy dwelling place. And that means no static thing. God is not static. He is the selfsame, always in act and always at rest; His very peace is dynamism, and His dynamism is peace.

If we enter the Church, if we let the Spirit dwell within us, then we ourselves are with Abraham on the mysterious Mount Moriah, hearing the voice of the angel, and seeing the ram caught in the thicket; and we are with the awestruck Moses before the burning bush, taking the sandals off his feet; and we are with David dancing naked before the Ark of the Covenant; and we hear the cry of John in the desert, and we sit with Jesus upon the hillside, and we eat from the basket of bread and fish that never is exhausted; and we stand with Mary Magdalene at the tomb, wide-eyed, and wonder what these things mean; and we hear the rushing of a mighty wind in the upper room as we pray with Mary and the Apostles; and we sing with Francis, and we pray with Dominic—and we march under bright banners, and what man can tell where we will go? But wherever it is, it will be with the Lord, who is the Creator and the Redeemer and the Sanctifier of time.

Chapter 5

If You Open That Door,
Nothing Will Be the Same

When the boy Jesus was twelve years old, He and His parents
went up to Jerusalem to celebrate the Passover, along with a
caravan of their kinsmen. Jesus must have been the sort of boy
who, although not necessarily talkative, was interested in other
people and might well have spent a day away from Mary and
Joseph, tagging along after an uncle or looking after some young
cousins. That is why it took some time before Mary and Joseph
noticed that He was not with the caravan. So they returned to
Jerusalem and found Him in the Temple, asking and answering
questions among the men—as brave and alert boys have always
done and, if given half a chance in our world that scorns them,
will still do.

We know that Jesus was from His conception always at one
with the Father. Yet in assuming our human nature, He assumed
also our weakness. The eternal Word had to learn to speak. The
hand that stretched the heavens like a tent had to hold to His
mother to take His first wobbling steps. And Jesus, raised in
that quiet and pious home, learned the difficult art of reading
the Hebrew script, most of whose vowels are unmarked, so that
the voice was needed to puzzle out the words as one went along.

But on His walks alone into the hills—for we must believe that He did as a boy what we see Him later doing as a man—He must have meditated in silence upon the Scriptures, upon the prophecy of Isaiah of the coming Prince of Peace, of the suffering servant who would heal his people by the lashes upon his back, upon the great psalm of dereliction and hope, with its cry, "My God, my God, why have you forsaken me" (Ps. 22:1), and upon the greater psalm of victory, "This is the day which the Lord hath made; we will rejoice and be glad in it" (Ps. 118:24).

What it was like to be that boy, we cannot really tell. The philosopher Jacques Maritain said that Jesus lived in patient expectation, not yet preaching to His people. He was waiting for the Father's time. And even when Jesus began to preach, He had to wait for His closest friends to catch His meaning. When the apostle Philip asked him to show them the Father, Jesus shook His head and looked upon him with disappointed patience. "Have I been so long time with you, and yet hast thou not known me, Philip? he that hath seen me hath seen the Father" (John 14:9).

But we are slow to learn. If it were entirely up to us, we would stroll our blind and heedless way to perdition. That is why God in His mercy strews that way with dangers—most of all, with the stories of those who have come before us. It's as C. S. Lewis once said, thinking about his own journey to the faith, that a man who wishes to remain an atheist has to be especially wary about what he reads. For every work that is steeped in the truth may open a door in what we think is the "real" world, and we may glimpse, through that doorway, the mountains of God.

So it happened to a young man who had lived a life of worldly ambition and dissipation. He was searching for the truth, so he opened the Scriptures, but he could make nothing of them. Not then, anyway—for he was looking for elegant Latin constructions, for the glare and glitter of sophisticated rhetoric. Later on he would see that he had been too proud, and that the word of God, that most dangerous of life-giving words, was like a vast palace with a low and humble door, approachable by children and simple people, yet having riches within infinitely beyond the imagination of the most learned. Still, he remembered the experience, and one day he found himself at Mass, when the homilist, a man of impressive learning and yet more impressive humility, taught his congregation about the mysteries hidden by God under a veil of allegory, just as Jesus had taught in parables, so that those who sought would find, but those who were possessed by scorn, who had neither ears to hear nor eyes to see, would never understand. And it was as if a new world opened out to the young Augustine.

He came to believe all that the Church teaches, but he was still enmeshed in sexual sin. He had not the strength to give it up forever. He prayed, "Lord, make me chaste, but not yet!" In agony one day Augustine wept, after he had heard the stories of simple, ordinary men who gave up far more. They were two praetorian bodyguards at Trier near the western frontier, who were well on their way to becoming "friends of the emperor," important men in the state. Then, on an idle afternoon, they opened a book on a table. And there they read of Saint Anthony of Egypt, whom I have mentioned, and how, upon hearing Jesus' plea to the rich young ruler, he sold all he had and retreated to the desert to lead a life of prayer and love of God. At once the guardsmen cried out, "Why are we leading this life? To what will it come, at best? How much better it would be if we lived for God alone!" Then and there they determined to become monks, and their brides-to-be determined in turn to enter a convent.

"How is it that so many people, even children, can enter, and I cannot!" Augustine, weeping, hid himself in an enclosed garden nearby, and there on a table was a collection of the letters of Saint Paul. While he was pleading with God, he heard a voice as of a child, calling out: *Tolle lege, tolle lege* ("Take up and read"). A perilous suggestion, that! So Augustine opened the book on the table and read the first words his eyes lit upon: "Let us walk honestly, as in the day; not in rioting and drunkenness, not in chambering and wantonness, not in strife and envying. But put ye on the Lord Jesus Christ, and make not provision for the flesh, to fulfill the lusts thereof" (Rom. 13:13-14). And it was, at once, as if he had died and been reborn, and from that moment his heart was at peace.

One winter night three men were walking in the woods beyond the school where they taught. They were talking about folktales they loved. One of them, an atheist, remembered when he was a boy, first reading about the Norse myth of Balder, who was the best loved and most handsome of the gods of Valhalla. But the evil Loki, seized with envy, tricked the other gods into shooting a deadly arrow at Balder, who perished on the spot. And the gods wept, "Balder, Balder the beautiful is dead!" When the boy read that, as unadorned as the story was, he too wept, with a strange sorrow that was somehow more precious than most pleasures. Why was that? The atheist could not say. But he argued, not happily, that the account of the death of Jesus in the Gospels was like that of Balder. Why should he believe the one, when he could not believe the other?

Then the friends of this C. S. Lewis—the great medievalist and novelist J.R.R. Tolkien and the critic Hugo Dyson—said something that Lewis did not expect. They fully granted the power of the myth of Balder. More than that, they affirmed that man had been made by God to be moved by such a tale, because in an unseen way it corresponded to the truth. We are, one might say, like bells attuned to the Lord. When we hear a story that is somehow in the Lord's key—even if we do not know it to be so—the music stirs a sympathetic response from our hearts. The old tale, said Tolkien and Dyson, was like a "good dream" granted to the pagan men of the north, as other good dreams had been granted to the Greeks, of Hercules the friend to man, or of Oedipus the cursed, with his mysterious and redemptive suffering. And it was as if the last piece of a puzzle had been put into place, or as if a new light had shone upon all the poetry that Lewis had ever loved, from the pagan Sophocles to the Christian Dante. He had been, as he would put it years afterward, "surprised by joy."

We talk a great deal of nonsense about education, when mostly what we mean is that children should be trained up in a dull secular conformity. We don't often think of the mystery of a child's first glance into those fields of wonder lying in wait behind the cover of a book. But God, who deigned to make a simple woman of Galilee into the mother of the Church, her whom we call our Lady, Seat of Wisdom, may go even further and deign to use the great stories of man to open our ears to the one and only story, that of salvation.

I remember a time of great darkness in my youth, when I wandered into a course in Shakespeare. It was taught by a man of profound Christian faith, but I did not know that at the time. I assumed that the professor was an unbeliever, as all of my other teachers seemed to be. But he showed me that the stories of Shakespeare resonated with the story of Christ. There is a moment, for example, at the end of the dark comedy *Measure for Measure* when a young woman, a novice of the severe sisters of Saint Clare, is called upon to plead for the life of the corrupt official who had attempted to seduce her and who she believes has been responsible for the death of her brother, condemned by a disused law against fornication. The very title of the play recalls the words of Jesus, "Judge not, that you be not judged. For with what judgment ye judge, ye shall be judged: and with what measure ye mete, it shall be measured unto you again" (Matt. 7:1-2). And by the judgment pronounced by his own lips, Lord Angelo now stands himself condemned to death. But Angelo's betrothed, Mariana, begs Isabella to say something—to say anything—to save the man. What will happen? Will revenge call out for rigid justice? Will the law somehow open out toward mercy? Will the man of sin receive what he deserves? If we each received what we deserve—if the Lord should mark iniquity, who would stand?

And Isabella falls to her knees, and begs for mercy for her enemy.

The secular world knows nothing of such mercy. And I, sitting in that class, saw, more clearly than I ever had, the terrible beauty of the revelation of Christ. My life has not been the same since. I have heard, too, of similar stories. Indeed, many young men and women have sat in my office and have testified to the power of the truth, presented in the form of a hauntingly joyous tale.

One young man, who arrived at our school as what he called "a card-carrying skeptic," told me that everything had changed for him. "How could it happen otherwise?" he said. "You guys have all the ammunition. You have Dante and Shakespeare and Cervantes and Milton! We don't have any defense against them." I rejoiced the following spring to witness his baptism into the Church.

We may suppose that a child who is formed by the great Story will "grow in wisdom and understanding," as Jesus did, and that is certainly true. But if we mean that he or she will leave the wonder of childhood far behind to become that dreary thing, an adult that scorns the childlike, then nothing could be further from the truth. In the opening of Shakespeare's *The Winter's Tale*—the greatest play of resurrection ever written—one of the characters, a king visiting his boyhood friend far away from home, is encouraged by his friend's wife to tell stories of their youth together. "Fair queen," he says, they were such as did not believe there would be anything "but such a day tomorrow as today, / and to be boy eternal." Of course, we know that the boy's sense of timelessness will fade. Our gray hairs and stiff knees will prove it. But is there no way to "be boy eternal"?

I recall the youthful gladness of my professor, who knew that most of his colleagues thought that his faith was quaint, but who knew better than they did that their own up-to-date faithlessness was old and humdrum stuff. I recall the youthful gladness of another mentor of mine, later when I myself was a teacher of the Story, and I would visit him in his office to regale him with one of my small victories, and he would laugh with me, as a father would laugh with his son. Or I think of the young men and women who visit me, with their bright eyes and their infectious enthusiasm, and I come to the grateful conclusion that there is no profession as fine as that of a teacher.

The Lord gives us plenty of time to grow young. How will we see the Lord, when we see Him for the first time? How can we tell? Saint John says that we will see Him as He is. But how is that? Is it unthinkable that we should see Him in the midst of a story? What would it be like, I wonder, to be walking in the mountains, delighting in such a day today as yesterday, singing, climbing rocks, looking to the incomparable skies, when all at once one should come upon another boy, with glossy black hair and a wise and playful smile, and then spend the afternoon talking of the Father? When Jesus spoke before the elders in the Temple, they were astonished by His speech. I should like to think that at least one of those old teachers so loved Him in his heart that he yearned to be a boy again at His side, to talk, and to learn, and to feel the presence of the Lord, the Lord, who gives joy to our youth.

Chapter 6

The Hidden Life

"The kingdom of heaven," said Jesus, "is like to a grain of mustard seed, which a man took, and sowed in his field: which is indeed the least of all seeds: but when it is grown, it is the greatest among herbs, and becometh a tree, so that the birds of the air come and lodge in the branches" (Matt. 13:31-32).

Again, said he, "The kingdom of heaven is like unto leaven, which a woman took, and hid in three measures of meal, till the whole was leavened" (Mt. 13:33).

Note that word *least*. Note that word *hid*.

A spirit stood at the marchlands between heaven and hell, taking instruction from a blessed Guide. All at once he beheld a shimmering of light through the branches of the trees, as if from the glancing reflection of a lake below. But it was no reflection. A train of joyful beings came into view, boys on one side, girls on the other, scattering flowers and singing to the strains of musical instruments. "If I could remember their singing and write down the notes," he said, "no man who read that score would ever grow sick or old." Finally came the lady in whose honor they sang and played. Whether she was naked or clothed, he could not remember, but if she was naked, her courtesy and joy, like a robe, gave him the illusion of a "great and shining train that followed her across the happy grass," and if she was clothed, her seeming to be naked was but the clarity of her soul shining through the robes and transforming them into her joy.

At first the spirit thought she might be Mary. He dared not utter her name. "Is it? ... Is it?" he whispered to his Guide.

"Not at all," said he. She was only someone the spirit would never have heard of, a certain Sarah Smith, who lived in the unremarkable village of Golders Green. She did nothing on earth that made the newspapers. But the history of the world as heaven knows it, and the history of the world as is written in books, are two different things. This Sarah Smith, says the Guide, was "one of the great ones." Every man who met her loved her, yet returned to his wife with greater faith and kindness. Every boy who met her felt her love, and became her son, "even if it was only the boy that brought the meat to the back door." Every girl became her daughter. The very animals of the fields about her house, the cats and the dogs, were touched by her life, and in her, said the Guide, "they became themselves."

It is a scene from C. S. Lewis's brilliant novella *The Great Divorce*. It has much to teach us, if only to return to the words of our Lord mentioned earlier, and to the reality of the life He lived, the hidden life, all those many years before He set out to preach and to heal, and to suffer and die. The mistake that the narrator makes, believing the woman to be Mary, is most fitting. For Mary too was, in the eyes of the world, a woman of no account, only an ordinary hardworking wife in a village in the outlands of Galilee. We do not revere Mary *despite* this lack of worldly achievement. The worldly achievement is neither here nor there. We revere her because her whole life was one of bearing the Lord within her, as she meditated upon the Scriptures in her girlhood, then bore the Son of God in her womb, and then, in the home that was like a place of meditation and like a womb, fed Him and cared for Him, and taught Him, and loved Him. When Jesus searched for a parable to describe the kingdom of God, no doubt He recalled His mother quietly working in that home, as any mother would do, kneading the leaven into the dough, as she had kneaded the word of God into her life.

And did not Jesus resemble His mother in this? If we look into the countenance of Mary, we see her Son. Hers is the face, says the poet Dante with stunning simplicity, "that most resembles Christ's." If we look into her life in Nazareth, hidden from us but fruitful beyond our comprehension, we look into the life of Jesus then, also hidden.

We should not suppose that Jesus' ministry for us only began when He left home and preached the good news of the Kingdom. Recall the parables. The kingdom of God is like a mustard seed. The kingdom of God is like leaven. In the recesses of the earth, in the unseen interior of the dough, in the quiet home, in the womb, in the heart of the holy family at prayer, the kingdom of God is present and at work.

I know a brilliant man who studied microbiology at the most prestigious scientific school in the world. Great things were predicted of him. To this day, I am told, the people who work in his old laboratory mention his name with reverence. But when he was there he would fall into conversation with the janitor, and that man, whom he calls the wisest man he ever met, changed his life. The scientist I am speaking of became a Dominican priest, and I hope he will not mind the praise if I say that I, in turn, have been leavened by his wisdom and his love and have seen them doing their quiet and wondrous work in the hearts of our students. Just as the leaven reaches every particle of the dough, and as the small seed gives itself wholly to unfold into the lovely tree, so the goodness of a simple man who cleaned the floors, a wise and unknown man, has touched the lives of people he never met: my life, and the lives of my students, and perhaps, like a far ripple of blessing, your life also, my reader.

We teach our children these days that they may do big things when they grow up. We do not teach them that they should do small things. We teach them that if they work hard they may become the idols of their peers. We do not teach them that idols are empty and foolish, that all their light is but glare, and all their music but sound and fury.

It is a common enough temptation, to mistake the big for the great, and to forget the lesson, taught again and again in the word of God, that He works His wonders by the most unregarded of instruments, for "the stone which the builders refused has become the head stone of the corner" (Ps. 118:22), and the Lord has chosen "things which are not, to bring to nought things that are" (1 Cor. 1:28). We may recall the words of Jesus, comforting to those who are unregarded, but dire for those who bask in the light of worldly importance: "I thank thee, O Father, Lord of heaven and earth, because thou hast hid these things from the wise and prudent, and hast revealed them unto babes" (Matt. 11:25).

Consider the history of the world from the vantage of the saints. It is the late nineteenth century. The intellectuals of the republic of France pride themselves on their skepticism. Ernest Renan, most famous literary dilettante of his time, writes a life of Christ that discounts His miracles as the fables of a backward and credulous people. The Jews had a tradition of learning reaching back hundreds of years, but let that pass; note the snide sense of superiority in Monsieur Renan. Bismarck has provoked a war between France and the Prussian empire, a sort of test run for World War I. Yet in reality the most important happening on a given day might have been that an ordinary middle-class man and his wife were taking their many children to Mass. How many millions of lives have been touched, or transformed, by the example and the intercession of young Thérèse Martin, now honored as Saint Thérèse of Lisieux? One can in fact trace a line from Thérèse to the Catholic novelist Leon Bloy, outspoken champion of the poor and the unregarded, and from Bloy to Jacques and Raissa Maritain, who were his godchildren when they entered the Church, and from the Maritains to their close friend Ernest Psichari, one of the first French heroes of the World War, who laid down his life in gallant action on the battlefield, covering his men as they retreated from a German onslaught. Ernest Psichari was named after his grandfather, the same Ernest Renan.

Christian poets have long given us stories wherein the destruction of evil is brought about by means of an unconsidered instrument — a child, an apparent weakling, a lone woman; wherein the good that is powerful but deeply hidden comes to light. In Tolkien's *Lord of the Rings*, the evil Sauron, swaddled in dreams of total power, overlooks the simple Hobbits of the Shire, and one of them, the young Frodo (with the indispensable assistance of his friend and servant, Sam, and the providentially employed greed of the creature Gollum), casts away the ring of power in which Sauron has placed all his vain hopes. In Dickens's *Tale of Two Cities*, it is the lonely and unsuccessful Sydney Carton, moved by the beauty of a pure and innocent young girl whom he must love, as it were, from afar, who gives his life to save her husband from the guillotine. As he walks in line toward his death, he comforts a little seamstress, whom

Dickens does not even name, speaking to her of the life beyond and sharing with her the last few minutes of his Christian love on earth. It is the love of a man most surprisingly *recalled to life*. Raskolnikov, the vain student in Dostoyevsky's *Crime and Punishment*, murders a vicious old woman pawnbroker because his theories of good and evil, which he wishes to publicize, give him the "right" to do so. While he justifies the murder to himself, and struggles to evade the arm of the law, a simple girl named Sonya, condemned by her drunken father and her sickly mother to sell her body in prostitution, prays for him and will be his salvation.

"There is nothing hid," says Jesus, "which shall not be manifested" (Mark 4:22), and perhaps we can conclude that it has pleased God to allow His most glorious works to be hidden, because only then will we begin to understand that He is Lord not of the great and powerful in the world, but of the small and the poor. For, says Mary, "He hath put down the mighty from their seats, and exalted them of low degree" (Luke 1:52).

I was speaking to the young men of an Opus Dei house near Harvard. That, one would say, is an important place to be, and I suppose I was speaking about something important, though I cannot now remember exactly what it was. We enjoyed plenty of pleasant conversation afterward, but what I remember most clearly was something that my friend and host said before leaving. "Let's go and visit the Lord," he said, and so we entered the small and silent chapel, where a candle was burning, and where the Blessed Sacrament dwelt, for adoration. Not only was that chapel "hidden," so to speak, in the bustle and the happy chatter of the house, but Jesus Himself was hidden, both present to view and hidden, under the simple appearance of bread. I felt, when we entered, close to my friend and close to God.

The Hidden Life

Those who believe that the "real" work of a Christian is the sort of thing that makes it to the newspapers have not stopped to consider the mustard seed and the leaven, and the Host in the monstrance or the tabernacle, and the presence of Jesus in the womb of Mary and in the home at Nazareth. Yes, there is the hour of the public celebration, and Jesus Himself began His preaching with the half-secret miracle of turning water into wine at the wedding feast at Cana. But we also have Jesus retreating into the desert, Jesus taking a boat to the far shore away from the crowds, Jesus climbing the mountain of Transfiguration with only three of his friends to accompany him, and Jesus alone in the unspeakable time between His death and Resurrection, harrowing hell, as people used to say, and setting free the souls of the men of old who had awaited His coming. The Jews of His day expected a son of David to come and lay waste to their Roman overlords. We smile at that misunderstanding, yet we think exactly the same sort of thing when we praise the prominent and forget the unseen, when we hearken to noise and stop up our ears against the silent, and when we plan great deeds for the Lord, while forgetting—I do this all the time—to tend to the small and near, to do the dishes, to play with a child, to listen to one's spouse, and to fulfill the unremarkable duties of our work.

I like sometimes to enter a church when no one else is there. Shut the door, and the world outside fades away; all you can hear perhaps is the low drone of cars on a highway or the chirp of a bird near the window. We are likely to think, "Outside those walls—that's where the real stories are unfolding, that's where life is being lived." Is that true? Within those walls, it is as if there is a heart beating, the heart of Jesus, who longs to give us life, and that in abundance. The windows tell of His time on earth, the relief sculptures on the wall follow His path up to Calvary. The altar is draped with the symbols of the Last Supper he shared with His friends, the Cross above shows the agony of love. And it all points beyond, to what? The tabernacle behind the altar, in the center.

What is a tabernacle? The word, literally, means "tent," that simple and small shelter against the hot desert days, the bitter desert nights, and the harsh desert wind. Outside, desert; within, welcome and love. For God has deigned to dwell among us, really to "pitch His tent" here. Why has He done so? So that we, in turn, might come to that tent not made with human hands, what the psalmist calls "the house of the Lord" (Ps. 23:6), what the apostle John calls the New Jerusalem. There is the true act, there the consummated story.

"Come, follow me," said Jesus to His disciples. What was that like? Imagine that you are Saint Peter, by his own confession "a sinful man" (Luke 5:8), living the energetic and dangerous life of a fisherman on the Sea of Galilee. Then Jesus comes along to call you away from that, to make you a fisher of men. It is a call to belong to a greater story than Simon can imagine, but surely it could not have looked like that at first. Jesus was, to all appearances, only a man. Jesus needed food. He needed a place to lay His head. If Simon had wanted to bustle against the Romans, he could have joined those movers and shakers called the Zealots—now *they* were certainly seeking a victory that the world would never forget! Imagine that you are Simon, young and irascible, and this Jesus, from nowhere but Nazareth, calls you away from your living, not to join an army against the invaders, but to join *Him*. Was it really the obvious choice to make, if you wanted to be an important player in the story of Israel?

The Hidden Life

Wouldn't it be like what happened to Martin of Tours, the soldier, when he met the naked beggar on the road and divided his military cloak in half to shelter him from the cold? When in a dream the beggar revealed himself to be Jesus, Martin heard the call to leave the great world of military conquest to enter the small world of monastic retreat, and all that happened was that Martin became the most revered saint in ancient Gaul, the bishop of Tours and the founder of monasteries everywhere. How could Martin have foreseen it? "My thoughts are not your thoughts," says the Lord to the people of Israel, "neither are your ways my ways" (Isa. 55:8).

"God resisteth the proud," says the apostle James (Jas. 4:6), and we think that that is their punishment, when actually it is simply a contradiction to suppose that it could be otherwise. God is goodness that desires to give of Himself to the uttermost. But He cannot give a gift to one too proud to receive it. So it is that in our pride we make ourselves too big to fit under the lintel of the church door. We would scrawl our name in great letters across the pages of the book of life, and we don't notice that in doing so we keep ourselves from ever entering the story of that life. Imagine a brigade of noisy and important men jangling their way down the alleys of Nazareth. So many are the things they have to do! So loudly will their praises ring from the throat of the legate of the procurator for the proconsul of the disease-addled emperor in retirement at Capri! And they pass by the home where Jesus and Mary live, and there is a light in the window. And all it would take—all it does take—is for one to leave the noise, and come into the silence. Then would his true life begin.

Chapter 7

Come In Out of the Rain

The crowds were gathering at the river. In one sense, they were leaving their homes far behind, to acknowledge their sins and be immersed in the water by the prophet in this place out of the way. But they were also returning home, to the wonders that God had wrought for their people and to the just worship of His glory. For when we sin, it is as if we try to leave home and go forth alone, like the prodigal son in the parable, or as if we were to lift ourselves in isolation out of the story of salvation. But there is no place outside of that story; as there is no water in the desert. So to repent is to turn home. And home is where the people are, not one by one, but *as one*, in a family, in a community, in the church.

So Jesus arrives at the riverside, and John recognizes him and cries out, "Behold the Lamb of God, who takes away the sins of the world!" (cf. John 1:29). We hear those words so often, but what do they mean? When John referred to Jesus as the Lamb, he was placing Him at the center of the story of the people of Israel. When they suffered the bondage of Egypt, the Lord instructed them to sacrifice an unspotted lamb, a male, and to sprinkle its blood upon the cross of the posts and lintel of their doors, so that the destroying angel would pass them by as he struck down the firstborn of their taskmasters. Every spring henceforth they would keep the memorial of that night, not alone, as we isolated modern people might, but in families, with neighbors, as a whole people. If Jesus is the Lamb of God—God, who has made Himself our Lamb, to give Himself to us in a sacrifice of love—He calls us to join Him as a new Israel, to be partakers of the shared warmth and joy of a feast, and no longer to wander like the sole lost sheep in the wilderness. That explains why, when John at first hesitates to baptize Jesus, the Lord advises Him otherwise, "for thus it becometh us to fulfill all righteousness" (Matt. 3:15). Jesus came not to destroy Israel, but to redeem it and make of it the great gathering of people from all the nations.

I know a man, now departed in the Faith, who spent most of his adulthood believing in nothing. He was an engineer of notable achievements, well paid, with a large family, and a devoutly Catholic wife. But when they went off to Mass on Sunday, he stayed home alone. Then suddenly, in his middle age, he was struck with a deep and terrifying depression. He spent time in a hospital. He searched for answers, first among the psychologists, then among the sociologists, but did not find what he was looking for. Or perhaps I should say *whom* he was looking for. When he found Jesus, he did not find Him as a lonely wanderer in an empty land. He found Him in the Church. For this man, who was my good friend and one of the keenest thinkers I have ever met, understood that man is made for communion.

The old saying, *extra ecclesiam nulla salus*, "outside of the Church there is no salvation," is not a legalistic formula to condemn people who have not heard of Jesus. It is instead a statement of fact about man, and God. God Himself is a communion of love, and if we are to be made like Him, then we too must enter the communion of salvation.

But there is something about this communion that my friend understood deeply, even fiercely. And that is that there is no such thing as a communion without obedience. He had lived for many years by his own lights, just as we are all encouraged to do in a world of alienation. Once he left his place of work, he was his own boss, and chose what he wanted to do. He had experienced the emptiness of that choosing. Then he saw in the Church a last bastion of sanity, of obedience to authority, without which there can be no body. For in our day we fail to understand Saint Paul's message about the body. The hand cannot despise the foot, but the foot does one thing, and the hand does another. The head cannot despise the belly, but the head does one thing, and the belly does another. "Are all apostles?" asks Paul. "Are all prophets? Are all teachers?" (1 Cor. 12:29). All are equally members of the body, but the equality is made manifest by the virtue of obedience. That means that the head "obeys" by leading, not for its own benefit, but for the good of the whole, and the foot, striding to battle, "leads" by obeying.

My friend looked out upon the wasteland of modern life, a life deprived of the nourishing fount of authority, and turned home — where, like that same prodigal son, he would put himself under the direction of a superior and would therefore belong to a genuine community, and not just a collection of separate individuals who happened to enjoy one another's company.

Shakespeare is the consummate playwright of authority. When the good earl of Kent is banished by his overhasty lord, King Lear, he returns in disguise as a peasant and appeals to the king for the opportunity to serve him. When the king asks why he would want to do that, Kent replies that he sees something in him that he would eagerly call "master." "What's that?" asks Lear. "Authority," Kent replies. We are meant to sense that that is right and proper, and that, regardless of the king's hot temper and foolishness, England would be far better off if her dukes would search that king for authority and obey it, rather than scrambling up power for themselves.

In *The Tempest*, the rebellious servant Caliban—reduced to servitude because he had attempted to rape his master Prospero's daughter—believes that he has cast Prospero aside and gotten himself a new master. It is a drunken and cowardly butler, but Caliban does not know that. Instead he kicks up his heels and sings out, "Freedom! High day! Freedom!" But Shakespeare understood that genuine freedom is impossible without obedience to a rightful authority. We obey the Lord, and those whom He has placed in legitimate authority over us, or we obey the evil one below. If we obey the Lord, we are free; if we go our own way, we are enslaved to the father of lies. The true authority submits himself to the good of those he leads; the tyrant fools those he rules by giving them a semblance of liberty and shackling them all the tighter. The true authority, and obedience to it, liberates and thus enables communities to be born—because our freedom is meant for our neighbor, in love, and not for our isolated selves. That too Shakespeare understood well. We see it in *The Tempest* when the young Ferdinand and Miranda pledge their love to one another. After Miranda has offered to become Ferdinand's servant if he will not take her for his wife, the young man kneels:

> *Ferdinand.* My mistress, dearest,
> And I thus humble ever.
> *Miranda.* My husband, then?

Ferdinand. Aye, with a heart as willing
As bondage e'er of freedom.

Their love is born not of an insistence upon equality, which is shot with envy, but of a recognition of superiority *in the other.* And thus they begin their marriage, a communion of love.

And the great community called the Church is unique upon earth! Think of it. When you go to Mass on Sunday, consider that hundreds of millions of people all over the world, city folk and country, people who teach at universities and people who cannot read a word, young and old, men and women, cranky and pleasant, saints and sinners and people still muddling through, are doing the same, are hearing the same words, are praying to the same Lord, and are remembering the same evening, when He sat down to sup for the last time with His friends. And a thousand years after our bodies have returned to the dust, unless God in the meantime shall have seen fit to bring our comedies and tragedies to their momentous consummation, people will still be falling to their knees when the priest repeats the words of Saint John the Baptist, "Behold the Lamb of God, who takes away the sins of the world." There will still be the priest, called upon to lead us, to minister the sacraments, and give us spiritual counsel, and pray at our sides when we are dying. There will still be the great stories of obedience that our betters, our authorities the saints, have given to us, the stories that we now have, and many more. There will still be the Pope, the successor of Saint Peter and the vicar of Christ on earth, to ensure that we remain as one, and not as the people of Israel in the time of the judges: "In those days there was no king in Israel; every man did that which was right in his own eyes" (Judg. 21:25). Here is what sacred Scripture says about such rejection of all authority: "There is a way that seemeth right unto a man, but the end thereof are the ways of death" (Prov. 16:25).

Return with me to a time in some ways like our own. It was a time when the old pieties of country and home had fallen into disuse. Monks themselves reflected the disorder. They became what were called vagabonds, literally men who were fond of wandering here and there. If a monk became dissatisfied with one house, he would simply turn up his nose and betake himself to another. In reality, it was simply a grand refusal to obey, to recognize authority. No one knows the names of such monks now. Why should we know their names? In their disobedience, they removed themselves from the true community. And when they did that, it was as if they had lost themselves, or erased the stories of their lives from the great story, the one that makes each of our stories true and lasting.

But one man saw into the heart of the disorder. His name was Benedict. He wrote a pious and well-balanced rule for monks, one that averted the danger of self-will. The monks were to take vows not only of poverty and chastity, but of stability—meaning that they must devote themselves to a single house, a single blessed place, to work and pray and live and die among their fellows there, and not wander about in the incoherence of their desires. They also vowed to obey the monk elected *abbot,* or, literally, "father." And what did these monks then do? The world about them fell into ruins; the great city of Rome became a ghost town, its renowned Forum a field of dilapidated temples and streets overgrown with grass, where stray dogs roamed and sheep grazed. The learning of the ancient world would have fallen into oblivion in all the western lands, but the monks, whom God was weaving into the history of his Church, preserved that learning, copied ancient books, and began to establish schools. That is, when they were not clearing forests, draining swamps, preaching to heathen tribes, sowing fields with corn, keeping livestock, ministering to the sick and the poor, and being the seed from which Christendom would spring.

For the truth is that we are made for obedience. When we find someone worthy of our allegiance, someone whose person stands for authority, we follow with good cheer, if our hearts are in the right place. I recall that when my father died relatively young, I had no idea how I would miss him. My wife and I had gotten married only a few years before, and now we had a child, and somehow I was to train up that child in goodness and truth, and provide for my small family, all without the counsel of my father. And I remember one day coming from a class on Saint Benedict and thinking, "What I need is an abbot!" Since that time I've sought spiritual counsel from the Dominicans among whom I work. I know too well that when I go off on my own, things begin to taste like dust and ashes.

Jesus was obeying the Father when He went to John to be baptized, even though He had no sins of which to be cleansed. He was setting us an example, and if He, who was sinless, obeyed, who are we to balk at doing the same?

Think of what happens when we do obey. My father was a good man. He sold insurance — mainly life insurance and disability. He worked not the nearby city, but the countryside, where homes were far apart and where, apparently, there were many fewer customers to call on. But he always found the country people to be hospitable, and he served them well, by his own obedience — to God, who demanded honesty of him, even when honesty meant that he told his potential customers that the policy they owned already was superior to his own. But that made him all the more firmly trusted. He became a part of their lives; his reputation spread about the rural counties. Old people would chat with him when he came by, and he in turn would sometimes pass their stories on to us.

When my younger brother was about to be married and was looking for a line of work, my father took him in hand, taking him on his rounds through the countryside, and teaching him how people should be treated. "Don't ever make a quick and dirty sale," he said, meaning that my brother should not just try to barrel into a house and overwhelm people with a slick pitch, disregarding their real needs—treating them as sources of cash, rather than real human beings with lives to touch. "It's like kicking a bag of manure. You may do it only once in a hundred times, but you'll never get rid of the stink."

My brother, whose personality is quite different from our father's, never forgot that lesson, nor the many others my father taught. He continues to obey my father, long after his death. This obedience is what causes him at times to tell stories of those car rides, when he was learning how to sell, and my father was carrying within him the cancer that would end this chapter of his life, the chapter among us in the body during these years in Pennsylvania.

When Jesus rose from the dead and appeared to his disciples, and then ascended to the right hand of the Father—whom He obeyed, and that is how the Son is equal to the Father, equal by obedient love—the disciples *then* began to understand His central place in the story of salvation, and the story of the whole world. Then they told stories about Jesus, reminiscing about what He said when the centurion was too embarrassed that Jesus should come under his roof, but instead confessed that he, a soldier who understood authority because he both commanded and obeyed, knew that Jesus had only to say the word and his servant would be healed. Or they recalled when Jesus sent the seventy-two out to preach through all Judea and gave them the authority to heal and to cast out demons. Or when He took them to the hill in Bethany, and, vanishing from their sight in order to be all the more present to their souls, He commanded them to take up the authority to baptize all nations, in the name of the Father, and of the Son, and of the Holy Spirit. They cherished the words of our Lord and recalled what He did, where He went, whom He challenged, and whom He comforted. They told these stories, faithfully preserving every least detail they could. In telling those stories, they obeyed the Lord and were fashioned by the Spirit into a Church.

At the end of Graham Greene's novel *The Power and the Glory*, a "whiskey priest," hunted by the communist officials in Mexico, especially by an idealistic and ruthless lieutenant, has finally met his death. He knew he was a sinner. He had been offered many a chance to lift himself out of the story of salvation. He could have renounced his vocation. He could have taken up with a woman of the streets, and "married," and been left in relative peace, as a constant sign of the supposed emptiness of the Church. But he would not do so. A small boy, whose mother loves the Church and tried to teach him its stories, had said that he wanted to be like the lieutenant instead. But when word comes around about the execution of the drunken sinner, the saintly priest, the boy's mind changes. The obedience—and there can be no real heroic love without obedience—moves him. And he asks his mother, in the end, "Please, Mama, tell us again the story about the saint."

"Seeing we also are compassed about with so great a cloud of witnesses, let us lay aside every weight, and the sin which doth so easily beset us, and let us run with patience the race that is set before us, looking unto Jesus the author and finisher of our faith" (Heb. 12:1-2). And from every witness there is a story, not one by one, isolated, self-made, but all together in one grand story, like notes in a symphony or the stones of a glorious cathedral. If we wish to be written down in the book of life, there is one way, and only one. We follow the example of our author and finisher, Jesus. We obey—we love.

Chapter 8

Turn These Stones into Bread

Soon after He was baptized in the Jordan, Jesus went out into the desert to fast and pray. After forty days of His fast, reminiscent of the forty years it took the Hebrews under Moses to cross the Sinai desert, Satan appeared to Him and tempted Him. "If thou be the Son of God," he said, "command this stone that it be made bread" (Luke 4:3).

"It is written, That man shall not live by bread alone," said Jesus, "but by every word of God" (Luke 4:4).

We are apt to think that the Devil was simply tempting Jesus to satisfy His hunger. After all, it had been a long time since the Lord had eaten. But it would not have been sinful for Jesus to eat a loaf of bread. In fact, after the temptation is over, and Satan leaves him for a time, we are told that angels came and ministered to his needs, just as an angel had come to Elijah on Mount Horeb, bringing him bread to fortify him on the journey he had to make. What, then, was the sin that Jesus was tempted to commit?

Perhaps we can see it more clearly if we consider the next two temptations. For Satan brought Jesus to a hilltop, and spread out before Him "all the kingdoms of the world in a moment of time." "All this power will I give thee," said Satan, "and the glory of them: for that is delivered unto me; and to whomsoever I will I give it. If thou therefore wilt worship me, all shall be thine" (Luke 4:5-7). That does not say much for the worldly power that men pursue. But notice the trap. Jesus must abase Himself, essentially to kiss the feet of the Prince of Darkness, in order to be "exalted" to the heights of that worldly power. It is a perversion of humility. When we humble ourselves before God, He does not simply raise us up by compensation. We are raised up in the very act of humility, because then we are most like the God, who made us simply because He loves us.

Then Satan leads Jesus to the pinnacle of the Temple, and tempts him to play God, as if Jesus could tug the puppet strings and make the Father dance. "If thou be the Son of God," Satan sneers, "cast thyself down from hence: for it is written, He shall give his angels charge over thee, to keep thee: and in their hands they shall bear thee up, lest at any time thou dash thy foot against a stone." But Jesus rebuked the Devil, saying, "Thou shalt not tempt the Lord thy God" (Luke 4:9-12).

The temptation was perhaps more subtle than we know. Certainly throughout Galilee and Judea there must have been many people whose insides were gnawed by hunger. Why not take the plan of God into your own hands, so to speak, and start writing the story yourself? Why not turn the stones into bread and feed the multitudes? Or look at all the kingdoms of the world, the Persians ruled by despots and their all-too-efficient bureaucrats, the Romans imposing law and peace upon their subject peoples at the point of a sword, the barbarian tribes beyond the Roman frontiers, living half by herding cattle and half by war and plunder. Why not, for the sake of all those suffering peoples, assume immediate lordship over them, and bring justice to them all?

But that would be like saying, "I, and not the Father, am going to determine the course of human history. And He will have no choice but to let me do it. If I should throw myself down from the Temple peak, He would have to save me. I will force His hand. I am the Author of life and light, not He."

When Jesus was a boy, the great emperor Augustus Caesar died. He had called himself the Prince of Peace and even had a famous altar erected in his honor to prove it. He boasted that he had found Rome in brick and left it in marble. After he had spent a few years having his political enemies assassinated, and once his rival Marc Antony was out of the way, Augustus attempted to reform the moral character of his people, passing laws requiring young men and women to marry, punishing adultery, and so forth.

Naturally, the astonishing accomplishments of Augustus—that was the new name, meaning "the one who brings increase," that a Senate of lackeys gave him—had to be memorialized for the world. So we have the famous statue of Augustus of Prima Porta, wearing leather armor and extending his hand in military command, despite the fact that the man really did not like warfare, and at the climactic battle of Actium against Marc Antony was sick in his tent, while his admiral Agrippa led the fleet to victory. And we have Augustus's "autobiography," a short tribute to himself, detailing all of the marvelous things he had done for Rome, and making sure that history would remember them.

Meanwhile, in a far and dusty province of the empire, Jesus of Nazareth, the true Prince of Peace, was growing in wisdom and understanding, and when He finally came forth in public to preach the Kingdom of God, He did not write down a single word.

There is a lesson here, but it is hard for us to admit it. Go into an airport, that clearinghouse of Important People. Stop at a newsstand or walk into a bookstore. Look at the magazines; scan the new hardcovers. You will find self-promotion everywhere. Some people promote themselves because they are rich. Others promote themselves because they say they love the poor. Some people promote their political prospects because they know that politics is the only real thing in the world. Other people promote their political prospects because they say they know that politics is *not* the only real thing in the world. Every cover fairly shrieks at us, in glossy smiling photos, "Notice me! I am smarter than others! I am better-looking! I am more caring! I can tell you how to live long, or enjoy fleshly delights, or amass a lot of money, or trounce your enemies! I am more than important! *I AM.*"

They might as well say, "See, I can turn these stones into bread."

Almost four hundred years after Jesus' Resurrection, the middle-aged Augustine, now bishop of Hippo in north Africa, who had once hoped to win a place of prestige in the empire by being a preeminent teacher of rhetoric, was persuaded by his flock to write down the story of what God had done for him. The result was his famous *Confessions*. People will say that it is the first autobiography in the history of the world. If Augustine had heard of such a thing, he would have been mortified; it would have been enough to keep him from writing it at all. For it is *not* an autobiography as we understand it. Augustine was telling the story of how God, the Author of all, had brought him to the truth, despite all of his foolishness and sin.

In fact, at several points in the book, we see people who think they have the strands of the story in their hands. For example, the practice in the Africa of Augustine's boyhood was to delay Baptism. The thinking was presumptuous, rather like the thinking behind someone's throwing himself from a high place with the assurance that God just *has* to save him. If you are baptized as a boy, the sins you commit afterward—and you are going to commit them, either because the grace of God is not in control, or because *you are*—will be all the more severe. Better to wait on the baptism, get all your sinning done first, and then, when you are old and the flesh has cooled off a bit, you can let the priest administer the sacrament. That would be to have your cake and eat it too. It is as if one were to say, "I can arrange even the spiritual details of my life as I see fit." Recall the man in Jesus' parable, who worked hard and achieved the Palestinian Dream, amassing an immense store of grain and saying to himself, "I will pull down my barns, and build greater; and there will I bestow all my fruits and my goods. And I will say to my soul, Soul, thou hast much goods laid up for many years; take thine ease, eat, drink, and be merry." But the Lord of time said to him, "Thou fool, this night thy soul shall be required of thee!" (Luke 12:18-20).

How silly were the idolaters of old, who knelt before the clumsy wooden figurines of their own making! We are wiser now. We kneel before mirrors.

But let us retreat from this madness. Let us return to Jesus in the desert. "Satan, begone!" he cries. And then He begins to preach the kingdom of God. It is the true and only story of our salvation, and He calls upon us to enter it.

That is what a little Albanian nun did, named Gonxha Bejaxhiu—her first name meaning "Agnes" in Albanian. She made her profession of vows, taking the name of Thérèse of Lisieux, a recently canonized saint known for her devotion to what she called the "Little Way" of holiness—that is, the way of spiritual childhood, of knowing that we have nothing to offer but the gifts of our Father. She went to India as a missionary, teaching at a girls' school in the fashionable city of Darjeeling, in the beautiful foothills of the Himalaya Mountains. She worked there for twenty years and was much beloved by the girls. But something troubled her. She knew of the terrible slums of the Indian cities, where destitute people would die like dogs in a ditch. She knew also that no one had dedicated his life to assisting them.

Then in 1946, on a train to Darjeeling, something happened. We would say that she made a decision. We would be wrong about that. If she had been writing an autobiography for a flashing and glaring newsstand, she would have recounted the story of her inner turmoil, the sadness she felt, the resistance to leaving the work she loved, and then, yes indeed, the triumph, with herself as the star of the epic, and all the grateful little poor people playing their cameo roles in her honor.

She did no such thing. She did not make the decision, but rather, followed the decision already made for her. She knew suddenly that she had to leave Darjeeling, as she put it much later, "to follow Him into the slums to serve amongst the poorest of the poor." She did not write this up. Indeed, she lived a life of great spiritual suffering, and kept it to herself and her priestly directors. She did not come with grand plans to cure all the diseases of India. She had no wand for making stones edible. Instead, she entered the lives of the people she came to love. With only a little food and medicine to give out, and hardly any money to spend, she began a school for the children of the slums. This she did, not by devising some new scheme to revolutionize education and make everyone rich. She did it by taking a stick and tracing the letters of the Bengali alphabet in the sand. And children came to watch—the children whose lives God would transform through her humble work.

That was Mother Teresa, the most famous and best-loved woman of the last century. Here is the great irony of it. Had she pursued a career of self-promotion, had she assumed that in her own hands lay the crafting of the story of her life, she would have been but another of the many thousands of self-promoters that flash a moment upon the stage and then are heard no more.

Everyone wants to save the world, but no one wants to do the dishes. I am thinking now of another saint. This man, Alfonso Rodriguez, a Jesuit brother, had a job to do in his priory in Majorca. He was the man who watched at the door. He did so for forty years. And while the Augusti of the world were doing the really prominent things, such as arranging assassinations and reforming public morals, Brother Alfonso led a life of quiet spiritual battle, with the grace of God conquering more demons than Napoleon did Russians, and being of more significance in the real story than were all those who earn chapters in the history books.

I am thinking now of two banquets. The one I'll call the Banquet of the World. Attending it, in great crowds, are the People Who Really Matter. Their stories have been written up in magazines with telling names, such as *Time*, and *Self*, and *Cosmopolitan*, and *Vanity Fair*, and *Salon*, and *Der Spiegel*—"The Mirror." Why, some people suspect that they have lived their lives only so that they could be written up in those places. They are the masters of their selves, like lemmings. When they speak to you, they look over your shoulder to see if someone more significant is hovering about. They eye one another askance. They are, however, united in knowing that only they can bring people together. They are the ones who have turned stones into bread. In fact, they chew at those crusts and pretend to enjoy the taste.

The other is the Banquet of the Lord. It is occurring right now, reader. All the newsmen and the photographers are at the first banquet, trying to shove one another out of the way. They are all trying to capture the moment, which is rather like trying to catch the wind in your fingers. But the second banquet is quiet. It is happening here, in this small church. The priest is elevating the host and repeating the words of Jesus, "This is my body." At this moment, time is steeped in eternity. We are there at the table with Jesus and the Apostles, and He is here with us, and we are all together with the saints and the angels, at the feast of the Lamb.

At the Banquet of the World, people marvel at their idols. The Important People stare into one another's eyes to see if they can catch a reflection of themselves. They cheerily announce their plans to save whales, trees, owls, troubled children, and the unnamed and unseen poor. They with their wondrous intelligence and goodness will prevent the earth from growing too warm or too cold, depending upon what year it is. They will save the little ignorant people from themselves, assuming the burden, alas so heavy, of governing them for their own good. And by the next day, it has all come to nothing.

But at the Banquet of the Lord, a quiet miracle occurs. The bread becomes flesh. Why? For the sake of still another miracle, one too small and insignificant to notice. It is that stones might become flesh—the stone of our hearts, which God has promised to take away, and give us hearts of flesh, whereon He will write His word, and He will be our God, and we will be made one, His people.

Chapter 9

Come, Follow Me

I remember once, when I was twelve years old and in a period of intense loneliness, I vowed to go a whole year without speaking to anyone in my school. That would have been one strange way to cure my trouble, and it was fortunate for me that the vow did not last more than a day. Still, I was awkward around the other kids. I didn't smoke, didn't pore over bad magazines, didn't ride a dirt bike, and didn't hang around the girls.

It took me some years to get through this feeling of alienation, and in college I made several close friends, with whom I shared a room for the better part of four years, with whom I ate lunch and supper, played touch football and threw the Frisbee, went to see movies, and argued about important things. In general we enjoyed one another's company.

That was a long time ago, and we are still friends, yet in a distant way. It isn't simply that our lives have grown apart, but that the "one thing needful" (cf. Luke 10:42) was missing. We did not worship together. We never said, "Come, let us sing unto the Lord: let us make a joyful noise to the rock of our salvation" (Ps. 95:1). What could substitute for our seeing in one another the image of the Lord? We never sang together, because there was no one to whom we could all sing. We knew fun, and that was a good thing, but we did not know joy. How could we?

I know a young man who enrolled in a prestigious school, who had no faith, and who therefore took up the substitutes of our time, using a drug or two, bedding down with a girl, working "responsibly" to claw his way to material success. It was all ashes. But there he met a chaplain. Isn't it instructive to us, how many conversion stories begin with a friend? He became a Catholic and then a priest—and from the day he entered the brotherhood of the Dominicans, he testifies that he has known only joy. It was as if he had come home. Or, much the same thing, as if he had left on a quest for home, in the company of his friends.

There's a calm moment of reflection in Tolkien's *Lord of the Rings* that bears some consideration. Frodo and Sam are making their way, alone, to the evil realm of Mordor, where they hope to destroy the ring of power by casting it into the volcanic crater of Mount Doom. Frodo had wanted to leave the others in their fellowship, because the ring was tempting at least one of them to evil, but Sam found him out and joined him, over his protests. In other words, this quest for the preservation of goodness is a quest of friendship. And Sam remarks to Frodo that they had long been used to hearing the old stories of heroism, yet never knowing what it was like actually to be in a story. But there they were, he said, in a story, whether they knew it or not, and we know, as we listen to their conversation, that without the simple love they give to one another, there would be no quest at all, and Middle Earth would be destroyed.

For the ancient pagans of Greece and Rome, friendship was the highest of virtues. It was surely accompanied by the feeling of affection, and made manifest in affability—say, having a drink of wine together or conversing together about the state. But it was more than that. The friend, said Cicero, is the man to whom you could speak your thoughts aloud. Aristotle said that friendship was not simply a sweetener to life, but the very purpose for which we establish a community in the first place. The great Socrates practiced his philosophy as a friend—often a prickly and ironical friend, but a friend nonetheless. So we see him retreating from the heat and noise of Athens with the young Phaedrus, to take their rest in the shade of a spreading plane tree and talk about the meaning of love. In the end, their conversation turns to the losses man incurs when he moves from dialogue to writing, and that might seem to have been tacked on by Plato, but it also is essential to his meaning. For philosophy was not a detached, academic discipline, to be pursued by careerists seeking to make a name for themselves, and some money. It was the pursuit of wisdom, and not in a lonely cell, but with other people—with the friend, with whom you could share what you had seen in contemplation.

There's a wonderful sacred romance of the early Middle Ages, written by an anonymous Cistercian monk, called *The Quest of the Holy Grail*. In it we are told that only the knights distinguished by purity will behold the mysteries of the grail, which was the cup Jesus used during the Last Supper, when he gave His blood to His friends as true drink. Those knights, Galahad, Perceval, and Bors, set out separately, as do most of the others, but the author brings them together on the Ship of Faith, and together, not separately, they will vanquish the ruler of an evil kingdom and be fed heavenly food. The final scene of the romance finds them together again, when a man from heaven clothed as a bishop descends to give Galahad the Eucharist from a golden chalice. Perceval and Bors, who have spent the last two years with him, look on as Galahad gazes into the chalice, and says, "Now I have beheld what neither eye has seen nor can the tongue of man relate." Those are his last words on earth.

It has never been granted to me to plumb those mysteries, but I do remember something of the *communion* of the sacrament, long ago when I was a boy, and we still knelt at the altar rail to receive the Host. For there you were, and as you glanced to the side you could see people you knew and people you didn't know, a cousin, an old man, a young girl, the neighbor down the street, the family of a classmate, all united on their knees, and often pausing to pray for a moment or two while the priest and the altar boy passed on to the next.

What more can I give my friend, but Jesus? Who else but Jesus can bind our friendship forever? When Saint Francis was beginning his ministry of preaching the gospel in poverty, a fervent young woman named Clare heard tell of him and asked him to come visit her. There began a friendship that had no equivalent in the ancient world. Clare herself began an order of cloistered nuns devoted to poverty and to preaching the gospel, and at times Francis would visit her, and who can tell of the conversation of those two, of what they saw and shared with one another? Chesterton imagined looking through a lighted window and seeing them there, the ardent countenance of the woman, framed in the simple headdress of a nun, and the fiery eyes of Francis, with his slight stature, and his angular jaw, the two of them leaning forward, laughing, or wedded in wonder. Evil people make alliances, not friendships, and then they break them when they are of no more use. Common people, in the ordinary ruts of sin, make friendships based on a shared pleasure, or a shared interest, and when those fade, so does the friendship. Saints become friends forged by the fire of God's love, which never fails.

And that friendship changes everything. It can change a life. It can change the story of the world. When the soldier Ignatius of Loyola lay in bed, recuperating from a terrible wound to his leg, he turned away from his worldly life to embrace the love of Jesus and the Church. Years later he would attract to him a small group of devoted men—his friends, the most prominent among them Saint Francis Xavier. Ignatius was not an especially learned man, nor was he possessed of a magnetic personality. Yet he was determined; he had fallen in love with Jesus; and love begets love. There is a stained-glass window of him in the church I attended as a boy. He is speaking with another man, probably Francis Xavier, who is dressed in colorful Renaissance regalia. The inscription reads, "What shall it profit a man to gain the world?" (Matt. 16:26). Those, of course, are the words of Jesus. But here they are applied in a double sense. Ignatius was pressing Francis Xavier to give up the world, in one sense—to give up his aims for a scholarly career—in order to gain the world for Christ. Ignatius didn't so much *persuade* Francis as *befriend* him. For love is a teacher.

That's what the great Saint John Bosco knew. When he was a young priest in Turin, he saw the untutored boys wandering the streets, falling eventually into lives of dissipation and crime. He felt called to minister to them—which is to say, to befriend them. He did not agitate for some soulless political program for the development of urchins. He went to them himself. Knowing that boys are attracted to the athletic, John Bosco did tricks for them. He juggled. He walked a tightrope. They were won by his kindness before they knew they were being won for Jesus. I have seen another stained-glass window in a nearby town, this time of John Bosco, his hands resting on the shoulders of a boy before him, the lad Dominic Savio, who died before he became a man, but not before he became the friend of John Bosco, and a saint.

Now let us recall those days at the beginning of Jesus' ministry, when He traveled near the shores of the Sea of Galilee and said to Peter and Andrew, and James and John, and the others, "Come, follow me!" What did He mean by that? Let us say first what He did not mean. He was not saying, "Come, be a proponent of the theological system that I shall unfold to you." That's the sort of thing we can do in our studies, writing bitterly satirical attacks on our opponents, and not winning the heart of a single suffering human being. He was not saying, "Come, listen to the interesting arguments I shall propose, and see if you find them rich or original." Jesus was, of course, rich—full of the riches of divine truth. As for His being original, in a certain sense He was, because the people had never heard teaching like His, full of authority, but Jesus Himself always says, "The Son can do nothing of himself, but what he seeth the Father do" (John 5:19), and "Think not that I am come to destroy the law, or the prophets: I am not come to destroy, but to fulfill" (Matt. 5:17). The men on the Hill of Mars in Athens, when Saint Paul preached there, were eager to hear new things—and that is probably the most silently damning thing said about anybody in the New Testament! That is because Jesus calls us by name, not so that we can sign a theological petition, or so that we can remain cool and distant speculators, turning our very inquiry into the divine into an idol. Perhaps that was Judas's mistake. Perhaps, when Jesus said, "Come, follow me," he had already turned Jesus into the leader of his own man-made system, a kind of reflection of Judas himself.

No, Jesus says, "Come, follow *me*." And that is highly unusual. The prophets did not do so. Elijah called Elisha away from his plow not to be his friend, but to be his successor. There were also, we are told, bands of prophets in those days, but we are not told anything at all about the band, and whether it was bound by friendship. As for the other prophets, they seem to be lone voices, with here and there a servant, as Elisha had the half-unfaithful Gehazi, and Jeremiah had his secretary Baruch. Isaiah did not gather about himself a chosen group of followers. Jeremiah did not, Ezekiel did not, Amos did not, Joel did not. Where do we most often find these men? We find Jeremiah, alone, cast into a cistern by his royal enemies; or weeping over the desolated streets of Jerusalem, destroyed by the Babylonians, with the people taken into captivity; or murdered by his enemies on their way to exile in Egypt. We find Ezekiel alone in the desert, beholding the great valley of the dry bones, and the foreshadowing of the resurrection. We find Elijah alone on Mount Horeb, crying out to the Lord to let him die, because he was no better than his fathers. We find Nathan alone, striding before King David, to convict him of murder and adultery.

But Jesus, when He returns from the desert, approaches those men — He does not wait for them to come to Him, but like the father in the parable, He sees them from a distance and runs to greet them. He says, commanding, pleading, inviting, opening Himself up to the embrace, or to rejection, "Come, follow me!" Scholars will say that Jesus, in choosing twelve men in particular, is reconstituting the people of Israel, giving them a new twelve tribes. If that is so, then it is a reform built not upon fleshly descent but upon a tradition of friendship. Jesus is calling those men to follow *Him*. We are Christians if we are in love with Jesus, and we show that we are in love with Him by following His commandments, the greatest of which is to love the Lord our God with all our heart and mind and soul and strength, and, the same thing in other words, to love our neighbor as ourselves.

Imagine two lives. One man has untold wealth. People honor him. He lives in a vast mansion on a mountaintop. He can have any woman he likes, at the snap of his fingers. His decisions divert the course of a nation's history. When he shakes his head, statesmen tremble. Yet he has no friends. Perhaps he does not even know that he has no friends, he has been so used to the flattery of people who secretly envy him and hate him.

Now imagine the poor little man of Assisi. He has nothing on his back but a burlap cloak. He eats little. He will never know the kiss of a woman. The leaders of his city think he is mad. No one trembles when he passes by. But he is consumed with the burning love of Jesus. That catches the eye of a man named Bernardo, and a man named Egidio — and they too want to join in that love, and they too throw away their shoes, and sell all they have, and join him, so that before Francis knows it, he is the leader of a band of brothers, of friends, united by their love of the Lord. Who would not choose the life of Francis, before the life of the successful and lonely? And we can choose that life, or something like it. We can enter that story. All it takes is a hearty yes. "Come," says Jesus, "follow me."

Chapter 10

Turning Water into Wine

In the movie *Tender Mercies*, a middle-aged man, who was a famous country singer before he took to drink, finds himself at a gas station in the dusty plains. He is looking for work. The young widow who runs the station, and who is trying to raise her small son to be like his soldier father who died in battle, has plenty of work around the place for a man to do. So she gives him a job.

The man has strayed far from his faith. He is a sinner, but he knows he is, and that gives him half a chance. For he begins to sing along with the widow — in church. They will be married, and in a gently comical but also deeply moving scene, the burly young minister baptizes him, in an immense vat of water, before the cheering congregation. The love of that good woman, who from the beginning has reminded him of the tender mercies of our God, has brought him home.

When we are baptized, says Saint Paul, we are no longer our old selves: "If any man be in Christ, he is a new creature: old things are passed away; behold, all things are become new" (2 Cor. 5:17). And what about when we marry? Why did Jesus first manifest his authority over nature in the miracle of the wedding feast at Cana?

Return with me to the beginning of the story. In that beginning, God made the heavens and the earth, and the Spirit "moved upon the face of the waters" (Gen. 1:2). What those "waters" were, we are not told exactly, but they were created by God, and from them, made fertile by the power of the Spirit, sprang all this glorious and spangled world we see about us, sun and moon and stars, mountains and valleys, seas and rivers, the glitter of snow and the fresh green of the springtime grass. But that was not enough. God wanted to give even more of Himself in love. So he said, "Let us make man in our image" (Gen. 1:26), and male and female He created them, and it is the first time in Scripture that we hear of this blessed distinction. They are made for one another.

How was this so? We are later told that God brought all the animals before Adam, that he might name them, thus exercising a God-like dominion over the creation has been placed in his charge. But there was no animal suitable for Adam. "It is not good that the man should be alone" (Gen. 2:18), said God, and He cast Adam into a deep sleep, and from his side—not from his feet, to tread upon; nor from his head, to domineer; but from his side, to be his indivisible companion—he took a rib, and fashioned it into a woman. And when Adam awoke, he saw Eve, and knew, in a flash of intellectual insight, that she was not like the other creatures he had named. "This is now," he cried, "bone of my bones, and flesh of my flesh!" (Gen. 2:23). Jesus Himself would turn our eyes to this moment, when he taught about the indissolubility of marriage. "What therefore God hath joined together," he said, "let not man put asunder" (Matt. 19:6).

If creation is the seed, then marriage is the flower. If in Baptism we are a new creation, then in Christian marriage that new creation comes to a flowering that the world does not really understand. The world drinks water, but the Christian spouses drink wine. In the world, the marriage marks the dedication of a man and a woman to one another in natural love, binding them and their families, and looking toward a future with children, and children's children. That is a holy thing. But it is incomplete. Water is good to drink, but the true celebration calls for "wine that maketh glad the heart of man" (Ps. 104:15). So in Christian marriage, when the man and woman leave their boisterous friends and relations, and retire to the holy temple of the marital embrace, they do more than recall the union of the first man and the first woman. They look forward to the unending feast, the wedding of the Lamb, when Christ and His bride, the Church, shall be one in glory. The poet Edmund Spenser had it right when he wrote a wedding poem for his own bride and commemorated that time when they were at last alone, but not alone, because the angels and the saints were present too. Their embrace was steeped in eternity, as they prayed for children, who would inherit "heavenly tabernacles," "of blessed saints for to increase the count."

So we turn to Cana, and we find Jesus with His mother and His cousins, and the first few of His disciples, and they are celebrating a wedding feast. It has not yet been revealed that we are all to be invited to a wedding feast incomparably greater, holier, and more joyous than this. Jesus has not yet compared the kingdom of God to a king who threw a feast for the wedding of his son, and the apostle John has not yet been granted the vision of the new Jerusalem, descending from heaven like a bride coming to meet her bridegroom. But there they are, and suddenly Mary—ever watchful for the welfare of others, with a woman's keen sensitivity, and with a mingled humility and motherly request—says to Jesus, "They have no wine" (John 2:3).

Let us pause here. "They have no wine." How can that be? When a young man and woman meet and fall in love, the skies are like opal, the sea like sapphire, the sunlight like diamond. Every favorite place is filled with meaning, as a vase with flowers. "Here is where we first walked on the beach." "That was the day I first met your brothers and sisters." "This is the diner where we first had lunch together." And on the day of the marriage, especially if they have not pretended to be married before they really were, it is as if all the revelers are present at the beginning of a new world. Out of all the men in the world, and out of all the women, they have chosen one another, and their children will be *their* children, unique and irreplaceable. They will, be it ever to so slight a degree, change the course of mankind. New stories will be written.

Do we not see it when we visit the homes of the elderly? My Italian grandmother had a big glass hutch that told the tales of her children and grandchildren. There they were, as babies, as gangly teenagers, as young people graduating from high school, as brides and grooms, and there were their children too; it was a running history of the family, with all the stories interwoven in the loves and the struggles that make up family life.

But in the marriage of the Christian, there is to be all that, and more. In that same hutch, my grandmother kept pictures of baptisms and first communions and confirmations. Above, on the wall, stood a studio portrait of her eldest, Teresa, who died of leukemia at age nine, on the very day when my father, her third son, was born. She had named her Teresa after Saint Teresa of the Child Jesus, the Little Flower. She kept the little girl's homework as a keepsake, and showed it to me at times, the old paper marked with a delicate and flowing script. The aunt I never knew, the sister my father never knew, was revered by all the family as a saint, and perhaps my father now sees her at last, joined in celebration. *That* is a story the world does not know how to tell.

So then, the people have no more wine. I doubt that Mary understands fully what she is asking Jesus to do. She knows that the hosts would be embarrassed by the wine's having run out, and that the revelers would disperse. The feast would end. Perhaps she knows, in a mysterious way, that she is asking Jesus to be a more profound part of the celebration; but she does not know that one day Jesus would bless the wine at the Passover feast and give it to His friends, saying, "This is my blood of the new testament, which is shed for many for the remission of sins" (Matt. 26:28). Jesus, who did know what He would eventually do, then performed the miracle that looks backward to creation and the marriage of Adam and Eve, and forward to the Eucharist, even the heavenly Eucharist of the Lamb. So He commanded that the stewards fill the big earthenware jars with water.

Again, there is nothing wrong with water. We need it for our life on earth. In the Christian life it is a means of spiritual purification. I look about and see it everywhere. I see a man and woman whose connection to Christ is weak, but who do love one another in a good and natural sense, and who do mean to begin a new life with one another, walking up to a ready-to-order minister for the occasion, and I see water. I see a young man graduating from high school and ready to leave his mother and father and embark upon a course of education, perhaps training for a well-paying and necessary job, but without any sense of a calling from the Lord, and I see water. I see the sweat of the laborer working to provide for his family, I see the natural tears shed by a loved one at a death. These are water.

Water is good. But the celebration requires more. It requires the Lord. So Jesus blesses the water, and then tells the servants to bring the casks to the chief steward, to let him taste of it. The chief steward does so, and then says to the bridegroom, almost in rebuke, "Every man at the beginning doth set forth good wine; and when men have well drunk, then that which is worse; but thou hast kept the good wine until now" (John 2:10). The good wine—not just any wine, but the good wine. The Lord Himself brings us that wine. The Lord Himself *is* that wine.

When my daughter graduated from our college, certainly there was, for some of the graduates, the thin and watery substance of a purely secular feast, one that looks backward a little and forward a little, but is not fermented with the yeast of eternity. But for many there was more. Many were drinking from the casks blessed by Jesus. One of them in particular, the valedictorian, gave a tremendous speech to the students graduating with honors. He recalled the stories of their lives together at our school, but he placed them in the garden of the time beyond time, reminding them that in Christ we do not lose these precious days of happiness together, but have them returned to us, glorified. In essence, the water of our days will be turned into wine, and that miracle is beginning even here, even now.

I recall our annual gathering in my house to sing Christmas carols. This year we had sixty people at least, young students with bright voices, old married men and women, college professors, neighbors, old friends. We crowded into our parlor around an old Canadian reed organ, the kind you have to pump with pedals and which makes a sound something like a recorder, something like a pipe, and something like an enormous harmonica.

Turning Water into Wine

We sang for an hour and a half. We sang carols from France and England and Germany and Sweden. We sang in four languages. One of our guests, who comes every year, said to my wife that she is sometimes so moved by the caroling that she has to leave the room, as her eyes grow misty. Perhaps, many years after my wife and I are departed, our children will remember those feasts and will continue them in their own families. Perhaps the students will remember, will place those feasts in the context of what they have learned at school, and will say, "Those were the years I learned what it is to be a Christian." We don't serve wine at our celebrations. Jesus, He it is who provides the punch.

That is the adventure and the blessed danger of inviting Jesus to the wedding feast—or, we might say, to any of our earthly celebrations, even to come along with us and a few friends to go fishing or camping, or to a ball game, but especially to be a member of the feast that begins the world again with a man and a woman pledging their love forever. Jesus will not simply be present at the feast. He will transform it. It will be a different thing in kind. It will be, so to speak, a moment in a story of infinite dimension. It is not like drinking water. It is drinking wine.

Chapter 11

Blessed Are the Poor

Jesus, strong in stature, His constitution toughened by years of the hard physical labor of His trade, and by His hale attraction to long walks, mountains, and the wilderness, climbed a hillside so that the crowds of people could hear Him. Among them were men, women, and children, the old and the young, the healthy and the sick, people who knew they were sinners, and people who didn't. And Jesus, in a voice that must have made the hillside ring, uttered words unlike any that men had heard before: "Blessed be ye poor: for yours is the kingdom of God!" (Luke 6:20).

I'd be a liar if I said I know what those words mean. We could spend the rest of our lives, I think, meditating upon this first and most fundamental of the Beatitudes and never come to an end of drinking of its wisdom.

That is, if we want to drink of its wisdom. The noblest of the pagans would have shrunk from it. Aristotle, a practical philosopher if ever there was one, held that to be really happy a man needed some wealth, not so much for comfort as for the pleasure of being generous with it. You can't be a great benefactor to your city unless you have some means. What he would have said about the poor widow whom Jesus praised, who gave her small coins to the Temple, and who therefore "cast more in, than all they which have cast into the treasury" (Mark 12:43), I am not sure. He probably would have praised her too—but to call her "blessed," that might have required a stretch of the imagination. Or more, infinitely more. It might have required the lifting of his human mind and heart to a new reality—as a sapling transplanted into another and brighter world.

But what do those words mean? Jesus was not sent among us to be a social worker, armed with a sheaf of strategies for eliminating poverty from the world. Indeed, He seems to suggest that that will never happen. "The poor always ye have with you" (John 12:8), says He. But that does not mean He is indifferent to the poor. Nothing could be further from the truth. He goes out to meet them. He feels deep pity for them. He inveighs against those who abuse them from their positions of prestige and wealth.

It is not hard to see Jesus' preference for the company of sinners as also a preference for the poor. For who could be poorer, or more miserable, than the tax collector in His parable? The Pharisee strides with insouciance to the foremost reaches of the Temple, where he contemplates the riches that God has showered upon him. He does not know it, but he is essentially falling down in adoration before man's favorite idol—himself. "God, I thank thee," he says, "that I am not as other men are" (Luke 18:11), for instance like the tax collector he noticed as he passed him by. And this Pharisee goes on to mark off, as a man taking inventory of his precious goods, all the righteous deeds he performs, as, for instance, giving to the United Way, and suchlike. Meanwhile the tax collector, "standing afar off, would not lift up so much as his eyes unto heaven, but smote upon his breast, saying, God be merciful to me a sinner" (Luke 18:13).

Blessed Are the Poor

Blessed are the poor, for theirs is the kingdom of God. Come with me to a prison cell. The most brilliant scholar of his day there sits at his desk, writing. He has been charged by his enemies with treason. It is essentially a political assassination. He is awaiting an unjust death, and, ever since the half-barbarian Goths came to be the overlords in the western empire, executions are horrible and cruel. Perhaps he knew what sort of death he would die, from having watched others. One account has it thus. His enemies soaked a leather thong in heated vinegar, to stretch it. Then they bound the man hand and foot, and tied the thong around his forehead. The thong would take a day or two to shrink, slowly, agonizingly, resuming its original size, crushing the bones and penetrating the brain.

So the man, Boethius by name, is writing. He pretends in his own person to be moaning the treachery of Fortune, who once blessed him with honor and now has taken everything away. But in the midst of his sorrow he is visited by a figure of surpassing splendor. It is Lady Philosophy. She will lead him back to the threshold of his true dwelling place. She does not say that the things that men pursue, such as wealth, fame, honor, power, and pleasure, are bad in themselves, but that they are only partial goods and that anyone who seeks them alone or even in combination with one another both gives himself over to the whims of Fortune and misses the true and unchangeable good he really seeks.

This is especially true of the wicked: for instance, those liars and power-grabbers who have conspired against this just man's life. "Consider how terrible is the weakness of wicked men!" she exclaims. They fail not merely in the quest for some earthly good, but in the quest for the greatest good of all, for the fulfillment of their beings as creatures who are made to love the good and the true. Consider, she says, that if God denies the wicked His mercy, He may allow them to continue in their ways, rich in the things of the world, and utterly destitute. For happiness, says Lady Philosophy, is not something that man can scramble up on his own, in measurable amounts. It combines in itself the goodness of all good things. It can be found only in God. Indeed, it is itself God.

What God gives, no man can take away. We can only refuse the gift. So Boethius, with his whole life snatched from him, awaited his execution filled with riches. He had been reduced to a poor prisoner in a cell. His enemies gloated. Yet just because he had the Lord, he had everything. As Saint Paul says, "If God be for us, who can be against us?" (Rom. 8:31). If the people of the nearby countryside are worthy of trust, Boethius died in a state of grace. They revered him as Saint Severinus, after one of his Roman names. His bones are honored in a tomb in the cathedral at Pavia, in northern Italy, where rest also the bones of Saint Augustine. His bones rest there, but his soul sings in Paradise.

Blessed are the poor, says Jesus, for theirs is the kingdom of God, and I look about my own home and say, "How can this be?" For I have worked hard to provide my family with good things—a comfortable and attractive home, and a cottage far away for vacations in the summer. And I look at the alumni whom my school—a genuinely Catholic school—most pointedly celebrates, and they are not housewives and plumbers and carpenters and janitors and kindergarten teachers, but those who have made a "success" of themselves in the world of business or medicine or, Lord help us, politics. Those are the stories we like to hear. We especially like to hear them about ourselves.

There is the danger. In one sense it does not matter how much we have in our bank accounts. Jesus did not come to preach the evil of personal property. That would be the companion error to believing that our salvation comes from property. "Except ye be converted," says Jesus, "and become as little children, ye shall not enter the kingdom of heaven" (Matt. 18:3). There is *nothing* in all the sagas and chronicles of the ancient pagan world that prepares us for such a saying; the closest, perhaps, is the sight of the aged and blind Oedipus, humbled by unspeakable suffering, led by the hand by a young girl, his loyal daughter Antigone. What can Jesus mean by it?

A little child has nothing of his own, but receives everything as a gift. This we can do whether we own a yacht and enjoy sailing it on the high seas, or whether all we can do is tie an old tire to a tree for our children to swing on. Is this what He means by the blessing of poverty? That we heed the word of Saint Paul, and buy, as though we "possessed not" (1 Cor. 7:30)? Is this the whole of it, that we do not set our hearts on such things, as if we were their masters? Perhaps. And yet there is the danger. "He hath filled the hungry with good things," says Mary, dwelling with joy upon the wonderful thing God has done for her, "and the rich he hath sent empty away" (Luke 1:53). The danger is that the things will stuff us full, and we will not be hungry for what really satisfies. The danger is that the things will be heaped so high that we will not see the vast homeland beyond. The danger is that the things will so distract us with their racket that we will not hear the still small voice that fairly broke the heart of the prophet Elijah.

But maybe there is more. Maybe I underestimate the very blessings of poverty. Let us engage in no sentimentality here. A life of poverty is not easy. It strikes fear into the heart of fallen man, as does the approach of the ultimate destitution, the thing we all fear. Says Dante, speaking of the young Saint Francis:

Reflections on the Christian Life

Still a lad,
Against his father he swept off to war
to win his lady love: and such was she,
no one for her unfastens pleasure's door,
As not for death.

Francis's father accused the boy of stealing money from the family till, to buy mortar to repair the local churches. Before the bishop and the town elders, in the public square of Assisi, he threatened to disown his son, but before he could do that, Francis disowned him instead, stripping off his clothing and tossing it back to him. That was his wedding embrace of the lady in whose honor he sang, Lady Poverty. Others fear her as they fear death, but, as Dante puts it with almost terrifying power, that Lady

was constant and so fierce
that when his mother Mary stood below,
she alone wept with Christ upon the Cross.

The world tells stories of people who work hard and go from rags to riches. It also tells stories of people who through their own folly or wickedness go from riches to rags. But Christians tell stories of those who through poverty—and often the material poverty we seek to eliminate—reap untold riches. This is not because we scorn the good things of the world, but because we seek what is above. Saint Francis himself, as that poor man of God, would fall in love all the more joyously with the beauty of the earth, even preaching to the birds.

This is hard for us to understand. A secular person might say, "Yes, I see what you mean. You are advocating a simple life, like the one that Thoreau lived when he retreated to Walden

Pond. Then he could appreciate the beauties of nature, and not be encumbered by the cares of the world." No, that is not it at all. Thoreau was animated less by love than by disdain. Sure, he was in a better position to love the natural world while living in a hut by the side of a lake than while living in town. But the joy of Saint Francis is missing. That is because Thoreau's self-imposed poverty was a protest against the way his fellows lived. Saint Francis, in his poverty, did not betake himself to the woods to escape the evils of Assisi. He preached in that town he loved, by his way of life. He was so obviously enraptured by his bride, Lady Poverty, that he attracted others to him, and soon there was a community, one whose spirituality would breathe in the art and poetry and song and life of the Christian West for hundreds of years. Thoreau died with a grumble; Francis, with a hymn.

Perhaps it takes a Christian artist who himself knew the pangs of hunger and the embarrassment of debt to help us to understand. The novelist Leon Bloy was a poor man with a family. He wrote fiery satires against the self-satisfied rich in France at the turn of the twentieth century and how they subjected the poor to indignity, squalor, thievery, and contempt. But in his novel *The Woman Who Was Poor*, we see the noble heroine Clotilde, after she has lost her infant son to disease, and after her beloved husband has laid down his life while saving others from a conflagration, give up everything and live as a beggar in the streets of Paris. She has known great suffering. Her mother tried to sell her off to prostitution. Her mother's bedmate was a filthy sot who once tried to rape her, with her mother's tacit consent. When her child died, an evil and debauched woman neighbor spread the rumor that Clotilde and her husband had smothered him. And yet she has the riches of Jesus. Has she been unhappy?

Her final words are simply these: "There is in the end only one unhappiness: not to have been one of the saints."

As the great Karl Adam says, "Jesus loves the poor not simply because they are poor but because spiritually they are more capable than the rich of hearkening to the message of the coming kingdom, of hungering and thirsting after justice." I imagine a palace atop a steep mountain. There is a legend that within that palace is unending and unquenchable joy. Every so often, a strain of music can be heard from it, but it is soon drowned out by the bustle in the plains below. Every so often, a radiance can be seen from its turrets, like the northern lights, but it is soon smothered by the glare of the shops and streetlights below. In the city of the plains, people bustle. You can read about them in the newspapers. Their stories sell. Their bodies sell, too, and sometimes the buyers won't have the story without a picture of the body. There is also a vast mart called an exchange, where people, jittery, breathless, hunted, suspicious, buy and sell stocks. Much of the bustle in this city on the plain is devoted to the elaboration of emptiness. You can buy emptiness in bright boxes. You can wear it on your shoulders. You can erect monuments to it. You can consume it, and in more than one way.

Now I imagine a young man at the base of the mountain. He has heard a distant echo of the strains of joy coming from the palace. He sees the steep narrow path that leads to the palace gates. It is called, by the city folk, the Eye of the Needle. They tell terrible stories about people losing everything who venture on that road—prestige, money, power, pleasure, and other objects of ultimate importance. All at once he sees a stranger before him. The stranger looks upon him with love. He says, "Come, let us go up to the altar of God." Now, the young man has a camel with him. The camel is heaped up with boxes. One box is full of diplomas, from the University of the World, Mammon Polytechnical, and Self-Lifting High. The young man is proud of them. He plans to use them to do good things. There is another bundle tied up with a rope. In it are pillows and blankets and sheets he has bought from an exchange called Astarte's Secret. The young man is taking them along, just in case. He isn't a dissipated fellow, not one to find himself ever feeding pods to swine, but he isn't a Puritan either. It is important to be prepared — that is what he has learned as a scout. Then there's a contraption with iron weights, for making his body handsome and strong, and a keg of beer, for doing the opposite. Medals, mirrors, letters from girls, pictures of himself, memories of victory, all heaped up on the camel, for the great adventure of life. This adventure, for most, means meandering about the plain, looking into the shops, dragging camels along, trying to keep the boxes from falling over, until the play is over.

"Come with me," says the stranger, smiling. And the youth replies, "I want to — I do. But what do I do with all my things?"

"You will lose nothing true. You may lose much that is untrue. We in the palace do not trade a genuine pleasure for a genuine pleasure. We cast away shadows and give what has substance. You can only gain. Aren't you hungry for it? Don't you thirst for it?"

"But what am I to do with my honors from the University of the World? I know I'm not the most important person alive, but I did think I would do something with myself. That was my plan, at least."

"Anything of truth you have learned there," replies the stranger, "you will not only retain, but you will find bearing fruit a hundredfold. But the chaff will be blown away. You must forget about honors. Think of your hunger instead. Think of joy."

"Maybe I can try to climb the pathway with my camel?"

"You may try, but you will fail. The poor beast cannot make it. This is not a path one climbs by being weighty and great. It is a path one climbs by being light and little. Take the boxes off the camel's back, and then lead him too, if you love him."

"I don't know... Can I think about it?"

"That isn't true, is it? You don't want to think about it. You want to think about something else instead. Come, isn't that so? Here, turn that noisebox off for a moment—I have a melody to give you. Or take down that neon light. I have a sunrise to give you."

"Why," says the young man, "you are a trickster! You don't want me to have less. You want me to have even more. You want to give me things. Why should I exchange these things for those things?"

"Because my gifts are true, and you know it. Please now, let's take these boxes and bundles off the poor camel. May I?"

What shall we do? Shall we let Him unload the stuff? He is waiting to give us all good things, if He can but find the room for them in our hearts. Why, He is waiting to give us Himself, if we would only come to Him as children. Blessed are the poor, for theirs is the kingdom of God.

Chapter 12

The Deaf and Dumb Spirit

While Jesus was at the top of Mount Tabor with Peter, James, and John, and His garments and His countenance became as dazzling as snow, something else was happening at the foot of the mountain, where the rest of His disciples were gathered. There was a man with a son plagued with a demon. Some people now might say that the boy suffered from epilepsy, for he would be cast to the ground whenever the spirit tore at him, and he would foam at the mouth and grind his teeth and, in the heartbreaking words of the old translation, "pine away" (Mark 9:18). But perhaps in this regard the ordinary people of Jesus' time were wiser than we, for whatever seized the boy seemed filled with malignity. The father explained to Jesus that sometimes it would seek to throw him into the fire or to drown him. And he pleaded with Jesus to have compassion on them, to do whatever He could do to help.

Do we know that poor lad? I believe we do. "The mass of men lead lives of quiet desperation," said Emerson. An overstatement, no doubt. Yet to live in this world is to know, at times, the helplessness of that father to protect his beloved son from harm, and the loneliness of the boy, who, when he is in the grip of the demon, can neither hear nor speak, but is lost to the world.

Reflections on the Christian Life

Retire to the stillness of your room, and reflect. I remember a year of darkness, its events almost wholly submerged beneath my memory, as if I had spent it entirely in the dim light of my college dormitory. I must have laughed at some time or another then, but when I think of that year, the image that comes to mind is of a map of the world covering one of the walls of our room, where students before us, young scientists on the make, had conceived the diabolical plan of amassing material for a nuclear missile and selling it to enemies of the nation. The map was pricked with the marks of thumbtacks locating possible customers. I remember attending Mass, not often, alas, at the campus chapel, an enormous neo-Gothic structure without the light or the rich playfulness of the great cathedrals of France, with the priest's voice echoing in the gloom; and I do not believe, in the hardness and the heaviness of my heart, that I ever heard a single word he said.

How difficult it is to speak of these times! The boy is thrashing upon the ground, insensible. The father looks on and can do nothing. The poet Wordsworth wrote of an old man, a farmer, who raised his grandson from a child and worked with the boy out in the fields, their last project the building of a great stone wall. The boy, Luke, eventually grew up, and sought to make his fortune far away, in the city. For a while he sent letters to the old Michael, but, like the prodigal in Jesus' parable, he fell into a life of dissolution, and the letters ceased. Michael, his body of an unusual strength for a man near ninety years old, would still go out to the place where he and Luke had last labored together. And there he sat, says the poet, "and never lifted up a single stone."

When my father's father died of a heart attack, his wife, whom he had spent his life ignoring and abusing, because he preferred liquor to love, was inconsolable. "Daddy, Daddy!" she cried, but the husband was no longer there, and the object in the coffin could not hear. In his novel *Vipers' Tangle*, François Mauriac writes of a successful lawyer with a terminal heart disease, who spent his years seething in resentment against his wife and their children. Louis writes his memoirs, expecting that his wife, Isa, will read them after he has died and after she and the children have carved up his wealthy estate, so that finally she will know who he really was. He wants her to see that he was not, deep within his heart, the monster they all thought, and that beneath the tangle of snakes that he and they both mistook for his heart there was a genuine heart, still capable of love. But Isa dies suddenly, and Louis, visiting her room, searches for something, anything, that would suggest that there was more than hatred between them. He finds parcels of letters, journals, burnt in the fire, with only a word here and there still legible. He learns that she had, for all those many years, lived with the quiet sadness of unrequited love. And now she has died, and there is no one to whom he can explain himself.

One of the saddest paintings I know, by the great Caravaggio, is of a young woman, buxom, sitting in a chair. Her dress is a touch on the fancy side, with lace and brocade, such as a woman would wear who plied the world's oldest profession. Some of the equipment of her trade lies on the floor: a jar of perfume, a broken string of pearls. She does not see them. She does not see anything. Her head is bowed, her shoulders huddled. Her hands lie in her lap, helplessly. Her lovely red hair looks as if it has been unceremoniously cut short. A single tear courses down her cheek. She is Mary Magdalene. Caravaggio knew the sadness, the loneliness that he painted so well. He sometimes painted himself into his works. In *The Crucifixion of Saint Peter,* for instance—as one of the soldiers heaving the cross to upend it; or in *The Supper at Emmaus*—as the inn-keeper, looking on while Jesus breaks the bread, looking on, and not understanding.

Or not understanding *yet.* For the people at the bottom of the mountain do not know what is happening above. But Jesus comes down from the mountain. We in our suffering do not climb the mountain to seek Him out. He is no solitary and self-satisfied hermit, dispensing advice now and again, and then returning to His icy calm. No, He comes to us. When Jesus met the father with the suffering son, He did not glow with light, as Moses did when he came down from Mount Sinai with the tablets of the Law. He had been transfigured before the eyes of the three chosen apostles, but now, with the scribes looking on, and the disciples who had been unable to drive the demon from the boy, He appears like a man among men, and one who knows our sorrows.

A friend of mine once said to me that his whole youth had been overcast with sorrow, because his father had abandoned the family when he was young, and he knew, although he could never say the words aloud, that his father did not love him and never would love him. And this heart's wound made it impossible for him to believe in God, until he met Jesus—in the face of a devout young man, his roommate at school.

Another man I know, in his seventies, radiates joy and peace, and lives in the strange freedom of having had all his choices taken from him. He is serving a life sentence, and the day they take his body from the walls of the prison will be the day, I trust, when he will look upon the walls of the New Jerusalem.

We do not hear, we do not see, we do not understand; we live in sadness, we live alone, and we fear that it will always be so. That is what the demon wants us to think. It is strange, says C. S. Lewis's arch-tempter, the devil Screwtape, that people always say that devils put things into their heads, when actually the devil's chief task is to *keep things out.* Imagine what would have happened if the father at the bottom of the mountain, hearing that Jesus was coming near, had instead clenched his teeth and gathered up his son and retired to his home. We think that we must knock at God's door, but God is ever knocking at *our* door, and the devils spend their time causing foolish and empty noise so that we will not hear. Their lie is to whisper, in our sorrow, "There is nothing more to life." Their lie is to snicker, in our loneliness, "No one draws near who will love you." Their tactic is to suggest to us that there is no story, and that therefore nothing or no one awaits us around the corner; no one is coming down the mountain to meet us.

But Jesus does come to us. He came to the grieving father, and asked the man whether he believed, and "straightaway the father of the child cried out, and said with tears, Lord, I believe; help thou mine unbelief" (Mark 9:24).

How deeply human the moment is! The disciples of Jesus had failed to cast out the demon. The scribes had looked on, asking them what they were doing, but being of no assistance whatever. When Jesus had heard of their failure, He rebuked them, saying, "O faithless generation, how long shall I be with you? how long shall I suffer you?" (Mark 9:19). The word *faithless* might well be translated as "unbelieving," so that when Jesus, in turn, questions the father, the poor man can muster up only a weak and unsteady confession of faith. He knows that he is no different from the people who have already failed. But he dares to go one step further. Surely it is his natural and blessed love for his son that moves him. He had begun by asking Jesus not for a cure exactly, but just for some help, and now he understands that he too is in need of help. To heal the boy is to heal the father. To cast out the demon is to cast out the weakness, the hardness of hearing, the insensibility. "Lord, I believe," he says through his tears. "Help thou mine unbelief."

In the spring of that dark year I returned home for Holy Week, and went to confession for the first time in far too long, and attended the Mass of the Lord's Supper, and heard, for the first time in my life, the great eucharistic hymn of Thomas Aquinas, the *Pange, lingua,* sung in procession by the boys and girls of the church's elementary school. I could have wept for the beauty of it, as they preceded the priest up and down the aisles, he holding the monstrance under the folds of his garment. I could have wept for my sins too, wept tears of joy, because they were forgiven, and I felt like a boy again. I imagine that Mary Magdalene, having turned away from her former life, knew times when the skies darkened again, and again she had to search for Jesus. "They have taken away my Lord" (John 20:13), she cries in anguish on the morning of Easter, when all along Jesus is there behind her, in the guise of the gardener. When the young man from the broken home saw the face of Jesus in the face of his friend, it did not mean that he would never suffer again. Indeed he underwent a terrible trial; but always the words of the psalmist were confirmed: "Though I walk through the valley of the shadow of death, I will fear no evil" (Ps. 23:4). Mother Teresa herself, having enjoyed the great gift of intimate speaking with the Lord and hearing His voice within her, was led by the Spirit into the desert of love, and for years knew only that beyond the darkness waited the Lord, who loved her so deeply that He would make her like Himself, thirsting upon the Cross.

The Deaf and Dumb Spirit

Consider again that contrast. Raphael has painted it in his *Transfiguration*. Beyond the vision of the people muddling through a life of sorrow, there is glory. We are as insensible to it as the boy in his raving is insensible to the cries of the people around him. But Jesus comes. And He asks us, while we sit at the dingy railway station, or keep watch over an aged parent dying in the loveless hospital, or return to a home where no one waits, whether we believe. He does not ask for perfect faith. He does not rebuke the father. He asks for something, anything. He asks for that fundamental act of trust, even in the midst of weakness. We recall the saying of the righteous Job, sitting on a dung heap, scraping the sores that afflict him from head to foot: "Though he slay me, yet will I trust in him" (Job 13:15).

Abraham, heavy of heart, climbed up Mount Moriah on that bleak morning with his beloved son, alone in his thoughts. And when Isaac asked him the question that tore at that heart — "Where is the lamb for a burnt offering?" — Abraham spoke perhaps more truly than he knew. "My son," he said, "God will provide himself a lamb for a burnt offering" (Gen. 22:7-8). The Lord will provide. The Lord is the Lord of time. The Lord is among us now. And He asks us if we believe, and when we place ourselves and even our faith in His hands, He is ready to show us but a foretaste of the glory we do not yet see.

For Jesus saw the boy in the grip of his debility, and all the people running about frantically. And He rebuked the foul spirit, saying, "Thou deaf and dumb spirit, I charge thee, come out of him, and enter no more into him" (Mark 9:25). At which point the spirit was wrenched from the boy, who collapsed to the earth in convulsions and then lay still, as if he were dead. But Jesus took him by the hand, and he arose. And when that happened—when Jesus raised the boy from the earth, did He not also raise the father from the spiritual sickness that had cast him down?

Lift up your head, and listen. Turn about, and see.

Chapter 13

The Pearl of Great Price

I wish to return to that moment on the mountain, when Jesus was transfigured before the eyes of Peter, James, and John. We may well believe that none of us in our wayfaring upon earth will be privileged to enjoy a moment so glorious. And yet I think that that is not exactly true. Listen to the words of Jesus: "The kingdom of heaven is like unto a merchant man, seeking goodly pearls; who, when he had found one pearl of great price, went and sold all that he had, and bought it" (Matt. 13:45-46). Doesn't Jesus imply that we are all searchers, like the man looking for pearls? And that there will come a moment when, to our astonishment, we will see "one pearl of great price," and then, if we dare to seize that moment of grace, we will sell everything just to possess that single pearl?

We are perhaps tempted by the clock to believe that in our lives time passes evenly and indifferently, just as the hands move, without pausing at any one moment. But that is not our experience. When the apostles saw Jesus transfigured on the mountain, they not only remembered it for the rest of their lives, but they interpreted in its light everything they were to learn about Jesus, everything they were to experience, and, most of all, His Resurrection. That is what Saint Peter is referring to when, as an old man nearing his martyrdom in Rome, he writes, "We were eyewitnesses of his majesty" (2 Pet. 1:16). Such moments shed their glorious light not only on what comes after, but on what has come before. Imagine what it must have been like in Jerusalem, after the Jews had returned from captivity in Babylon. They had to rebuild the walls. They had to rebuild the Temple. And they had to rededicate themselves to the Lord, who had promised them this land so long ago. So the priest Ezra gathered together all the people, the men and the women and those children old enough to understand, "and the ears of all the people were attentive unto the book of the law" (Neh. 8:3). The people wept. They knew that the sins of their ancestors had caused them to be cast out from the land, and now they had returned, and with all their hearts they wished to be united again with the God who had brought Abraham from the land of the Chaldeans, and who had miraculously freed the children of Israel from their slavery in Egypt. They wept. But this was to be a day of glory, not sadness. Said Ezra: "Go your way, eat the fat, and drink the sweet, and send portions unto them for whom nothing is prepared: for this day is holy unto our Lord: neither be ye sorry; for the joy of the Lord is your strength" (Neh. 8:10). And they kept the feast for seven days, as if they were celebrating the re-creation of the world.

They are moments of transfiguration, when the clouds open, and we see glory. They are not necessarily moments of what we would call pleasure. They do not fit into our lives, so much as our lives are fit into them, and that fitting can be violent indeed. When he was a boy, Dante says that he caught sight of a beautiful girl on the street, whom people called Beatrice or "the blessed one" even when they did not know her name. Nine years later, he met her again, and such was the overwhelming force of her beauty that he had a dream, wherein a majestic figure, carrying the sleeping Beatrice in his arms, looked to the young man and said, "*Ego dominus tuus*" ("I am your lord"). From this encounter with Beatrice, an encounter that set its roots down in the rich soil of the sensitive poet's soul, the whole of Dante's poetic career would derive its meaning: from the anguish of her early death, to his forgetting her and wandering astray into dubious philosophical speculation, to his return to her, which he casts as the result of her intercession on his behalf, saving him from himself, and returning him to the best of his youth. A young man sees a beautiful and saintly woman, and from that vision we have the *Divine Comedy*, and thousands upon thousands of readers catch a reflected gleam of "the Love that moves the sun and the other stars."

The joy — the wonder, the transfiguring light — works backward and forward, as we might well expect, since God is not bound to time, but is its Maker and Lord. I recall a sunny day in North Carolina, when I was a graduate student. I was walking across a great green field toward the main street of the town, when all at once it seemed to me that the whole world was right and beautiful, that everything was as it ought to be.

And I remembered, just then, with an overwhelming power and sweetness, a time when I was a little boy, visiting my grandmother who lived a few houses away, and who was cooking French fries in the oven, cut from the potatoes by hand, thick and white inside, and a little blackened on the edges outside. I remembered that boyhood time, and I still think of it now. My grandmother passed away many years ago, but if I have ever met a saint on earth, she was that saint. I used to think, when I was an arrogant student at Princeton, that there was something missing from her life, because she could not understand calculus, and I could. Such was my stupid vanity. But now I see that God gave her to me as my grandmother to help ransom me from that vanity. That moment of remembering was not *the* pearl of great price; it was not itself the kingdom of God. But it was a pearl nonetheless. I've pocketed that pearl. It casts its light upon my past. It helps to light my way for the days to come.

When the prophet Elijah retreated to the mountain of the Lord, he felt that all he had done had been in vain. Yes, he had proved the god Baal to be false and had slain his priests with the sword. But the wicked queen Jezebel still pursued him, seeking his life, and the people of Israel had not turned their hearts back to the Lord. So he cried out, "Lord, take away my life; for I am not better than my fathers" (1 Kings 19:4). But an angel of the Lord came to Elijah and told him to stand upon the mountain, and the Lord would appear to him. Then there came a great wind, battering the mountain and smashing the rocks, and an earthquake, and fire, but the Lord was not in any of these things. Finally came "a still small voice" (1 Kings 19:12), a little whispering sound, a gentle breeze, perhaps a word whispered into the heart of the prophet. And he hid his face in his mantle. It was from this moment, and not from his glorious battle against Baal, nor from his long and weary struggle against Jezebel, that Elijah would take the meaning of his life. This is the moment that strengthens him. And the Lord instructs him to anoint Hazael king of Syria and Jehu king of Israel, and Elisha to be his disciple and the prophet that will succeed him, and these three will bring judgment down upon the worshippers of Baal.

What is it like, to hear the still small voice? What is it like, to find that pearl? I've said that we cannot pursue the joy of these moments, just as we cannot compel the Spirit to shed His light upon our hearts. But we can *allow ourselves to be pursued.* The merchant in Jesus' parable had no power to create a pearl of great price. But he was looking for one. He was open to the possibility of finding, and, as Jesus says, "Seek, and ye shall find" (Matt. 7:7). Had Elijah been mingling with the noisy crowds, he might not have heard the voice. Had the old man Simeon been in a public house, drinking away his last few years, he might not have encountered Jesus in the Temple. That's not to say that the Lord cannot approach us there. After all, He struck Saul blind with his glory when the man was filled with his bustling plans to persecute the Church. But He Himself instructs us, when we pray, to retire to our rooms, as He retreated into the mountains and the desert, when He wanted most intimately to commune with the Father.

The enemies of the faith will try to persuade us that if we leave the noise and bustle behind, we will be abandoning our lives. They will say that the blazing glare of fame and power and wealth and lust is light in abundance. They will entice us to stand, not upon Mount Tabor, but upon some platform under the spotlights, and let those moments of glory suffice. But that is a lie. That platform is what Malcolm Muggeridge calls Legend:

> This is where history is unfolded and news is made; this is where we live our public, collective lives, seat and unseat rulers, declare wars and negotiate peace, glow with patriotism and get carried away with revolutionary zeal, enact laws, declaim rhetoric, swear eternal passion, and sink into abysses of desolation.... Those who belong exclusively or predominantly to the Legend are power-maniacs, rulers, heroes, demagogues, and liberators. In

extreme cases—Hitler, for instance—they bring about their own destruction. (*Jesus Rediscovered,* "Credo")

The fierce pleasure of victory over a rival will eventually give way to loss, as power is leached away by age and debility, and fame subsides into oblivion, and lust dwindles down into a dead coal in the grate. To live for such moments is to die. But consider again Saint Francis, the poor little man of God. He would often leave his beloved brothers to pray alone for a while in the mountains, and no doubt he knew moments of transfiguration there. Saint Francis, who owned nothing but the burlap cloak upon his back, owned the very world itself, because he had found a pearl of great price and had sold all he had to purchase it. So his eyes were opened on the quiet slopes of Mount Subiaco, and he could sing in praise of the beauty of all the creatures of the Lord.

Yet sometimes the moment may come to us in the form of a person. We do not know. When the three travelers came upon Abraham and his servants and their flocks, the good old man welcomed them and bade them sit down to eat and drink. We Christians have long seen in this moment the approach of the Holy Trinity toward Abraham, and it was then that the prophecy came to him that his aged wife, Sarah, would bear to him a son. The writer to the Hebrews, considering this moment, would recommend that we too practice the virtue of hospitality, welcoming the stranger into our midst, because in ancient times, by so doing, "some have entertained angels unawares" (Heb. 13:2).

Modern life, filled with noise but not with conversation, causes us to view one another as objects serving some function, like the machines on a checkout counter. But the Christian must strive to remember that the next person he meets may be bearing a pearl of great price. He may be the one sent by God to open for us the doors to the kingdom. It does not matter whether he is aware of it. Do we suppose that the merchant seeking pearls found what he was looking for among the hawkers at the pearl exchange? Perhaps someone came to him one day while he was simply sleeping in the shade.

We must be alive to that possibility. I cannot say I am particularly wise in this regard. I have the weakness of the teacher, who thinks that his task is to bring light to others, to cast pearls before them, if you will, and who therefore often forgets how needy he himself is. I'm tempted to think, "God has set me before these students to bring them some moment of light," and that may not be such a bad thing to consider. But while I am busy bringing light and congratulating myself for it, I may be missing the true light and may be forgetting that God has sent the students to me so that my own darkness may be dispelled. We do not know.

A few years ago an old man wrote to me to ask if we could meet for lunch. He had read some of my articles and was impressed. We became good friends, meeting once a month to laugh together, to talk about theology and philosophy and about the social organization of the modern world, which was something he studied most ardently. I learned later from a mutual friend that Don had been a physicist of prodigious accomplishments. He had, for instance, invented the diode that is in use throughout the world. He was a late convert from nothing at all to Roman Catholicism. There he would sit at our favorite restaurant, his six-foot-seven frame bent over with arthritis, wearing a trainman's cap from his beloved Steam and Wireless Museum, and beaming at me. I'd thought at first that he wanted to find out things from me, but it was exactly the reverse. He wanted to teach me what he suspected I didn't know, about Christian anthropology and the vanishing sense of awe. He was carrying a pearl.

Don died suddenly a few months ago. His children invited me to come to his house and take away a few boxes of books from his library. When I arrived there, I was stunned. Don had, after his dramatic conversion, bought thousands of books of theology and philosophy, and had read them too, as I could tell from the notes he made in the margins. He had, shall we say, that moment on the mountain of transfiguration and had come to see his entire life in its light, both the past, when he was an unbeliever, and the future, and the time beyond the future. I miss him, but I don't miss him, because that first time I met him is still with me, and I know that if God has mercy upon me, I will meet him again on that distant shore.

In our weakness we may complain, "If only I had been there upon Mount Tabor to see the Lord transfigured! Then I would be strong." Is that really so? And have we never been upon that mountain? Or, "If only three angels had knocked at my door! Then I would believe." Is that so? And has no one ever knocked upon our door?

I am writing this beneath a window, and the loud clear flute-like calls of an oriole are coming to me. The sky is a hazy blue, lovely beyond words. My dear wife is pottering about in the garden. Is not God offering me a pearl right now? Is that so hard to believe? Recall the parable of the mustard seed. It may be small, as a pearl is small, but it is also a natural thing, even, where Jesus lived, an ordinary thing. Perhaps when Jesus told the parable there was a mustard tree in plain sight, growing wild, with a couple of sparrows fluttering from bud to bud.

The Pearl of Great Price

Which is the way to Mount Tabor? Where is the pearl to be found? This is the moment that contains all moments. This is the day that the Lord has made. Look down at your feet, and see what God has placed in your path. Look to your neighbor, and see whom He has sent. Look up at the sky, and see the gleam of His glory.

Chapter 14

The Giver of All Good Gifts

"It is more blessed to give than to receive," says Saint Paul, quoting the Lord (Acts 20:35). Why should that be so?

Jesus and His disciples have retreated to a mountain overlooking the Sea of Galilee. The crowds have followed them there, and Jesus has showered a generous gift upon them, the gift of His teaching. But the day is growing late. His disciples are concerned for the welfare of the crowd. They were often like that; they seem sometimes to want to be Jesus' managers, looking out for the Master's comfort. Here they did not want Him to suffer the embarrassment of leading a crowd into the desert without any food. They were in favor of dismissing them, so they could find food in a nearby village.

Jesus turns the suggestion right back at them. Go ahead and feed the crowd yourselves, He says.

Andrew, who must have been an amiable fellow, one who paid attention to other people, brings a lad to Jesus and says, "There is a lad here, which hath five barley loaves, and two small fishes: but what are they among so many?" (John 6:9). Jesus then instructs the disciples to have the crowd sit down on the hillside, in groups. Then He takes the bread and the fish, blesses them, and gives them to the disciples to distribute.

What happened then? Some scholars used to say that the people were so abashed by Jesus' generosity that they took the food they were hiding from under their cloaks and started to pass it around too, until finally everybody had eaten his fill. There are several things wrong here. First, if people had been in the habit of carrying food with them everywhere they went, the disciples would certainly have known about it. After all, they themselves would have done so. They were not strangers in that land. Second, assuming that that was the case, why would the disciples have reported the event as a miracle? And not only on this occasion, but on others too. Were they fools? Then the disciples gathered up the fragments into big wicker baskets. Were those people who followed Jesus then expecting to make a great picnic of it, planning ahead for the occasion, and somehow concealing all that food? Did Andrew happen to notice one boy who had something to eat, but nobody else? Are we to believe that it didn't occur to him or to anyone else to ask, "Do you people have any food?" Wouldn't that have been the *first* question they asked? And wasn't the answer the reason they approached Jesus to begin with? And can we actually imagine that the Jewish people, as hospitable as they and Italians and other Mediterranean peoples still are today, needed to be shamed into sharing food?

No, Jesus, the Son of God, multiplied the loaves and fishes and fed the hungry. The miracle is a shadow of the great multiplication to come, when He would make Himself fully present at all the altars of the world, under the appearance of bread and wine, to feed the hungry still.

But let's return to that scene. There is one person other than Jesus who gave. It was the boy with the bread and the fish.

All the others gathered there would look back upon it as the day when they received something miraculous. Only the boy would remember it as the day when he gave something that turned out to be miraculous. And this bears some thought.

"It is more blessed," says Jesus, "to give than to receive." Certainly it can be made to appear more glorious. Cicero wrote a long epic poem, and not a very good one, commemorating his own heroism in saving the Roman republic from the rebel Catiline. Cicero was a deeply flawed but still fairly noble man. Yet it is perhaps just such a lover of mankind that Jesus was exposing when He said, "The kings of the Gentiles exercise lordship over them; and they that exercise authority upon them are called benefactors" (Luke 22:25). In ancient Athens, rich men considered it their civic duty to put forth the funds for staging plays during the great religious and patriotic festivals. No doubt their patriotism was mingled with family pride. They could say, "We're the family that financed Sophocles when he staged the play about Oedipus and the terrible riddle." We can, perhaps, come up with a timeline for our lives, calibrated by moments of conspicuous and public generosity. "Here is a picture of me ready to cut the ribbon for the new school building. Here is another picture of me at the Special Olympics. And here is a picture of me receiving an award for philanthropy from the governor."

I don't mean to look down upon such giving. But it seems not to be the sort that Jesus is talking about. After all, our Lord said that when we give alms, we should not let our left hand know what our right hand is doing. What, then, makes it more blessed to give, if we may not even feel better about it, and if we gain no applause from the world for it? Why is it better to be the boy with the bread and fish than someone in the crowd settling down upon the hillside?

We might say that to give is an act of love, and love enlarges the heart. When we are children, we remember, "This was the year my mother and father gave me my first bicycle. It was blue, and it had a bell and a horn, and I loved it." There's nothing wrong with such memories. They are all the sweeter because they are bound up with a gift, and not with something impersonal, something merely stumbled upon. So too we might say, "I gave my wife this grandfather clock for our twentieth anniversary, although we had to look around together for three years to find it!" I remember the day I asked my wife if she would marry me. We were in a rowboat on a small lake, with her terrier, Oliver. It was a sunny afternoon, and there were plenty of people about, but nobody near enough to overhear us. I believe we went to buy our wedding bands after that. And in fact it was a gift itself that won my heart. She gave me a musical instrument, a wooden recorder. Only someone who knew me well and loved me would have thought of it.

I still have that recorder, so many years later. Maybe that gives us a clue. There is something about the true gift that transcends time. It is not simply that we bask in the moment's glory. As long as I live, I will never give away that recorder, because it means for me a whole lifetime of love between me and my wife. She is, in a sense, still giving me that gift. It can never be exhausted. And that means that when we give, in love, we approach the heart of God, who gives eternally. Someone who gives, but only for a time, and with reservations, does not truly give at all; instead that form of gift is rather like a taking. It is at best a business contract, at worst a cheat. To say, "I will give myself to you as long as I love you" is to say, "I keep myself to myself and do not love you." To say to a child, "You can enjoy my support so long as you are under my roof, but when you leave, I'm living my own life," is to say, "You are an accident in time that has happened to me, and no more."

The Giver of All Good Gifts

To give as Jesus gives is to approach the eternal love. This is difficult for us to conceive. We are covetous of things, but most of all covetous of life, *our lives*, lived as we choose to live them. Sure, we will be generous when it suits us, but we will decide the where and when, the what and how much.

How difficult it is to let go of our schedule and dwell in the glow of eternity! Perhaps, though, we can take a lesson from the boy.

We don't know his name. That in itself is suggestive. Maybe it was Nathan, meaning "gift," or Jonathan, meaning "God gives." Maybe we will meet him in paradise and say, "So, that was you!" Yet this unnamed boy is the hinge of the miracle. For Jesus uses his gift a thousandfold, to give to others. Perhaps the lad got more to eat than he had started out with! That would have been quite a meal; but even if not, he gave *and he received*. He gave what he had to Jesus, and received from the Lord the incomparable gift of having been the one whom Jesus took to Himself to feed the crowds.

Mother Teresa never wanted anyone to write her biography. We can imagine a much lesser woman keeping a diary of gifts, with entries such as, "This was the day I broke ground for our first leprosarium." She did not do so, because she was instead committed to doing what she called "something beautiful for God." That meant that before she gave material aid to the poor of India, she gave herself to them, and she could only give herself to them because she had first given herself to God. And she gave herself to God, not believing that it was an act of her own overflowing goodness, which it was not, but in gratitude to God, the giver of all good things, who had given her so much. Even as she grew old, she seemed, as it were, beyond time, with that childlike glow in the eyes and in the smile that characterize people whom God has especially showered with grace.

We are all, then, invited to be the boy in the Gospel account. What we have to give is little enough in itself. Mother Teresa began with only a few rupees. Men and women about to marry begin with not much more than they had when they entered the world — a poor naked body. But when we give these few loaves and fishes to Jesus, He multiplies them. We shouldn't expect notoriety for it. Remember, we do not know that boy's name. But we will draw near to the eternal Lord, who told the woman at the well that he had "living water," water that quenches the thirst forever (John 4:10).

Jesus says to all of us, "Come, follow me." He does not ask us for contributions. He asks us for ourselves. *That* is the gift that is blessed, both in giving and in receiving. And this brings me to my final point, one that is also not easy to explain.

When someone gives us a gift in love, he puts himself at our mercy. The gift by its nature cannot be completed unless we receive it in love. Otherwise it is a mere transfer. No one guides his life by a transfer. So there is an inner harmony between the generous love and the gratitude, the giving freely, and the freely receiving. That is why Jesus says to His Apostles, "Freely ye have received, freely give" (Matt. 10:8). He does not mean that they owe it to their neighbors to give, as if they were repaying a debt. He means instead to convert their whole way of thinking about giving; He means to invite them into the life that He enjoys. This is a life of ultimate freedom, because it is a life of free giving and free receiving.

And what has God given us? He sustains every moment of my existence. He fills my lungs with air. He brings light to my eyes. I behold the marvels of a creation so beautiful that it makes me sorry to know that I must leave it someday, even though it will be for a new creation. He has given me a mind to see the truth and a heart to delight in it. He gives me love, through the people I meet, through my family, through the students I teach, and through many others I will not meet in the flesh, but who have touched my life—Saint Augustine, I am thinking of you. He does not cease to give. He is multiplying the loaves and fishes now. He is giving of Himself utterly in the Sacrament of the Altar, somewhere in thousands of churches as I write this sentence. He asks only that I receive Him.

But to receive Him is to give myself to Him. When the apostles led the boy to Jesus, I'm sure they had not snatched his food from him. The boy saw Jesus and had the opportunity to enter into giving and receiving, giving himself, and receiving a miracle in return.

It happened on a warm day nearly two thousand years ago. It is happening right now.

Chapter 15

The Crown of Thorns

When we recite the Creed, we declare that Jesus suffered for us unto death. We know that the suffering ended upon the Cross. When did it begin?

There was a man roughly contemporary with Jesus, a Greek slave named Epictetus. He was a Stoic philosopher of the popular sort, less concerned with physics and metaphysics than with how to live the life of a wise man. If you said to Epictetus, "Today you shall be put to death," he would reply, "And since when did I ever tell you I was immortal?" The Stoic ideal was to conquer suffering by scorning it. Epictetus affirmed that all things happened according to the design of a benevolent Providence. But that Providence was not a person to whom one could appeal. It was not love. So the wise man might relieve the suffering of his neighbor, if he chose, but it would be madness to *share* that suffering.

In this regard the Stoics were not so different from their despised rivals, the Epicureans. The great Epicurean poet Lucretius, writing several decades before the birth of Jesus, imagines a truly wise man standing upon a promontory, looking out on the hectic passions that motivate his fellowmen, and enjoying his detachment from them:

Reflections on the Christian Life

How sweet, to watch from the shore the windswept ocean
Toss someone else's ship in a mighty struggle;
Not that the man's distress is cause for mirth —
Your freedom from that trouble is what's sweet.

In the East, this form of enlightenment came one day to Gautama Siddhartha, now known as the Buddha, as he sat meditating in the shade of a tree. He saw that human suffering is all bound up with the cruel wheel of desire. The answer, he said, is to free oneself of the wheel, by practicing the eightfold path of benevolence and renunciation.

That is not the answer that Jesus gives. Indeed Jesus could never give that answer, because it is no answer. It is an evasion. Some of the most profound thinkers among the pagans saw that a life defined by detachment from suffering was hardly a human life at all. Plato shows us that love — born of plenty and poverty, of overflowing richness and passionate need — is our chariot in the quest for true wisdom. Cicero argued, against the Epicureans, that a man who did not enter into his neighbor's suffering could not be called a friend. They would have agreed with Jesus when He said, "Greater love hath no man than this, that a man lay down his life for his friends" (John 15:13). And yet in our suffering we do not turn to Plato or to Cicero, but to Jesus. Why is that? What, if anything, is our suffering for?

We are too ready to think that Jesus, being God in the flesh, would be protected from suffering, at least until the onset of His Passion and death. The exact reverse is true. Precisely because Jesus was God, He would feel with a keenness we cannot imagine all the wretchedness of sin, the stupidities that wreck our lives, the tearing of the heart at the moment of a loved one's death, and even the ordinary demands of the feeble body and soul. He was a lone innocent man in a world of sinners, as if He were the only man who could see color in a world of black and white, or the only man who could still hear music beneath a world of shouting, blasphemy, sniggering laughter, idle gossip, sharp-eyed wheedling, and groans. His suffering with us and for us and on account of us began the day He was born.

When Jesus goes into the desert to pray, before beginning His public ministry, He does not do so to leave his fellowmen behind. He wishes to be alone with the Father, so that He can then bring the people into a deeper relationship with the Father. He is like a soldier, preparing for the attack. So Satan tempts Him to flee from suffering, by fleeing from both the Father and the people of Israel. Is He hungry? Does He in His fasting share the gnawing ache of the poor? Let Him turn stones into bread. Is He weak, the son of a defeated people? Let Him assume command of all the kingdoms of the world. Is He the Chosen One of God, but unknown? Let Him stand atop the Temple, that symbol of Jewish might and Jewish shame, the Temple twice destroyed and twice rebuilt, and let Him hurl Himself off its parapets, to prove Himself. These are all the whisperings of the fallen creature we call Satan, the Accuser, the Adversary. If God is love, then the Prince of Lies must hate God's solidarity with the sinful human race. It was Satan who tried to pry Job from his devotion to God, and who, in the persons of the man's three "friends," accused him only, and spoke not one word of comfort. When Saint Peter reproaches the Lord for saying that He must go up to Jerusalem and be put to death by sinful men, Jesus calls him Satan—the very man whom He had just called the Rock upon whom He would build His church!

Jesus looks upon the people and has compassion for them, because they are like sheep without a shepherd. He looks upon

Jerusalem and says that He has longed to take her under His wing, but the people have refused. He regards the rich young man with love, inviting him to take that step beyond all the commandments, that step into complete dependence upon the Father; but the young man went away sad, because he had many possessions. He sees into the heart of Nathanael, the Israelite in whom there was no guile, and the fisherman Peter, who said that he would never abandon him — but Jesus knew otherwise. He has pity upon the woman caught in adultery. He is eaten up with zeal for the house of the Lord and makes a whip of cords to scourge the money changers from the Temple. He shakes His head with disappointment, wondering how His disciples can have been with Him for so long and still not understand what He says. He goes about the countryside preaching and healing, not wishing to call attention to Himself. When Martha says to Him, "Lord, if thou hadst been here, my brother [would not have] died" (John 11:21), He does not say, "Did you not know that your brother was mortal?" He does not scorn her. He weeps. Even the mourners said, "Behold how he loved him" (John 11:36).

Pope John Paul II once wrote that the purpose of suffering, for fallen man, is "to unleash love." It is a stunning insight into the economy of salvation. We learned, after his death, that the Pope wore a cord about his thigh, to mortify the flesh. It was a way of reminding himself of his creatureliness, and of expressing solidarity with all those who suffer. The aging pontiff, his mind sharp but his body broken with palsy, his once athletic and youthful frame hunched over, his face haggard and somber, stood as a witness to the dignity of human life, even in suffering. To deny this dignity is to reduce man to a thing, to be fixed when broken, and when he cannot be fixed, to be numbed, so as to pass away with least inconvenience to those around him. To die in a hospital ward, surrounded by the machinery of a business, with people about who care about your medications or your physical pain, but who do not care about *you*, seems to some people so inhuman that they prefer to cure the indignity by destroying the dignity itself, requiring doctors to kill them when they cannot make them live. It is an act of benevolence to alleviate someone's suffering. This can be done from the outside; a doctor can do so, without remembering the patient's name. But only love can *share* the suffering, and that can never be done from the outside. We must welcome the sufferer into our hearts. It is what Epictetus, for all his wisdom, would not do. It is what Job's friends did not do. It is what Satan can never do. But it is what Jesus came specifically to do. It was His Father's will. When He ate with His companions, when He trekked over the mountains of Palestine, when He healed the sick, when He comforted sinners and welcomed them home, He was doing the will of His Father, and opening Himself out in the wound of love.

And this, I believe, is the mystery of the crown of thorns.

When a Roman general was victorious in battle against the enemies of the empire, the Senate would sometimes vote for him a "triumph." The triumph was a parade through the city, sometimes entering beneath an arch specially built for the occasion. So, for example, when Titus, son of the emperor Vespasian, sacked the city of Jerusalem in A.D. 70, the Romans erected a colossal arch near the Forum, complete with relief sculptures showing the destruction of the Temple and the desecration of the sacred seven-lamped candelabrum. Behind the general would march his legions, along with the plunder they had heaped up from the conquered land, and the prisoners of war. Traditionally a slave would be stationed beside the general to whisper into his ear, "*Memento mori,*" meaning, "Remember that you will die." That was to keep the general from growing arrogant in his victory. It was as if to say, "If you begin to think of yourself as a god, you will end up like one of these miserable people led in defeat behind you." Yet that is worlds away from Christlike humility. The implication is that the loyal Roman general will be the cause of suffering in others, and will, if he knows his place, keep that suffering at a distance. The idea that he might suffer in his own turn is not an invitation of love, but a threat.

The crown of thorns shows us the infinite difference between hate and love, which is also the infinite difference between what the world thinks of power and glory and even of being itself, and the truth of these things, made manifest in Jesus. Recall the scene. The Jewish leaders, in envy, have thrust Jesus upon the hated Roman authorities, on the grounds that He called Himself their king. Note the perversion. The Jews had long been waiting for the Son of David, the Anointed One of God, to come to set them free from bondage and indeed to make Jerusalem the city to which all the nations would turn to worship. Were it not for the revelation of God, it is perhaps the most astonishing and even absurd claim that any nation has ever made. It is as if the people of some obscure island, some-where like oft-conquered Crete but not nearly so big, were to declare their land to be the religious center and consummation of human history. Well, that is exactly what has happened; but that is not my point here. The point rather is that for once the Romans and the Jews seemed to agree on something. They both considered a king to be the man who possesses power *over;* they saw the king's rule in terms of the subjugation of enemies. They were not entirely wrong. But the enemies were neither Rome nor Palestine, but sin and death, to be defeated by the burning heart of love.

Place yourself within the precincts of the Roman praetorium. Jesus has just been scourged. He has been whipped to an inch of His life by the cat-o'-nine-tails, a whip whose splayed ends are embedded with bits of stone, glass, and iron, to dig deep into the flesh and cut away muscle and nerve. There are rumors that the man is innocent. There are other rumors that He has claimed to be a king. You are one of the Roman guards. Your name, say, is Tertius. You are the third son of a middle-class merchant, so you have entered the army to make a little money and have some adventures. You have seen rape and pillage and can tell some stories about your own part in them. You have seen easily a hundred men crucified, and some women too. You've occasionally hammered the spikes into the hands and the feet. All legal, of course. You are not particularly cruel, after all. You once braved the arrows of the enemy to rescue a fallen friend on the battlefield. But outside of your platoon, your response to suffering is to ignore it, or to laugh. Now you see Jesus.

What is there about Him to mark Him apart from other men? You see no distinction, no beauty. He is just another ruffian from the Galilean hills. He made Himself a king, is that it? So you, Tertius, conceive of a bright idea. You do not share the man's suffering. You wish instead to aggravate it, and you will do so at some risk to your callous hands. You go to a bush whose thorns are an inch long, and carefully cut away several branches, which you plait into a crown. Then you press that crown down upon Jesus' head, the spikes digging below the scalp into that net of nerves and veins that cover the skull. Streams of blood flow down upon the face of the Lord. "Hail, King of the Jews!" you jeer, and you and your fellows beat Jesus with reeds.

Imagine the hundred thorns of that crown, each one penetrating the flesh of the Lord and issuing forth in blood. Each one marks an opening, a wound. What Tertius cannot imagine is that this is in fact the crown of a king. The golden crowns that oppressors wear are but paper and paint by comparison. Each thorn is a human sin, and each sin meets with the love that does not ignore our sins, as if we were of no importance, nor excuse our sins, as if God were a careless Father. It is a love that overcomes our sins, by sharing in our suffering—even taking upon itself the suffering we are too callous to feel. The love is kingly because it is magnanimous in the highest and Christian sense: the soul of Jesus is great enough to comprehend in its embrace every sinner and sufferer the world has ever seen. So Jesus spoke not one word of rebuke to the soldiers, but instead spoke on their and our behalf from the cross itself: "Father, forgive them; for they know not what they do" (Luke 23:34).

When the thorn presses, then, let us remember the Lord, and open ourselves out in love.

Chapter 16

My God, My God

On the night before He was to die, Jesus went up to a garden on the Mount of Olives to pray. He said He was saddened unto death. He knew that the hour of the apparent triumph of evil had come. Yet He did not strut and pose. He did not strike a heroic attitude, so as to impress His disciples. He knelt in the garden and prayed, "Father, if thou be willing, remove this cup from me: nevertheless not my will, but thine, be done" (Luke 22:42). Such was the anguish of His heart that Saint Luke, the physician, tells us that His sweat was like drops of blood.

There is a kind of courage that is born of pride and defiance. When Cicero heard that his arch-enemy, Marc Antony, had combined with Octavian in seizing power, he knew that his days were numbered. He made his way in a chariot from his country villa toward Rome. But he never made it to the city. The chariot was stopped along the way by Antony's men. Cicero, knowing what they were about to do, thrust his head out of the chariot and told them to be quick about it. He was beheaded instantly.

Then there is insensibility, which sometimes looks like courage. A Roman cohort that had disgraced itself in battle was subject to the rule of *decimation*. The men would be lined up at random, and every tenth soldier would be counted out. Then the soldier at his side would thrust a sword through him. It might be his own friend who would kill him. But the Roman veterans would have seen greater horrors than these. I doubt that any of the surviving nine or ten missed a meal or slept the worse for it that night.

And there is resignation, that sigh of hopelessness in one who has no faith. It is not submission to the will of God, but a shrug, an admission that things are bad, but can be no better. We see it often in people who are terminally ill, whose only wish is that death would come soon, and painlessly.

None of these is true courage, and none was available to Jesus on that dread night.

He could not die in pride and defiance. "Learn of me," He taught His disciples, "for I am meek and lowly in heart" (Matt. 11:29). He reminded them, again and again, that he who humbles himself shall be exalted, and the last shall be first, and unless we become as little children, we shall not enter the kingdom of heaven. Pride is the elemental act of hatred, because it sets one apart from one's fellows, and from God. But Jesus said, "Inasmuch as ye have done it unto one of the least of these my brethren, ye have done it unto me" (Matt. 25:40). Saint Paul, echoing an ancient Christian hymn, says that Christ did not think equality with God something to be seized, but emptied Himself, taking upon Himself the form of a slave, and becoming obedient unto death, "even the death of the cross" (Phil. 2:8). Instead, the death of Jesus was the fullest expression of His oneness with our deepest suffering, our feeling utterly alone, our severance from all we love.

He did not die insensible. "Father," He prayed from the Cross, "forgive them, for they know not what they do." Consider

how quick Jesus was to every glimmer of love, every motion of
the human heart, for good and for ill. Consider that Jesus again
and again calls us to feel more keenly the sharpness of sin. We
do not excuse ourselves for never having committed adultery,
when we look upon a woman with lust in our hearts. We do
not excuse ourselves for never having killed a man, when we
spit insults at our brother, calling him a fool. Jesus said that He
came to bring us life, and that in abundance. But what does
life mean? It is not the prolongation of our bodily functions. It
is being alive with the love of the living God. The Levite who
passed the man who had fallen among thieves was insensible,
and to that extent he was not alive. The Samaritan was alive.
The Pharisee who looked with scorn upon his brother in the
Temple, and who praised God for making him righteous, was
insensible, and to that extent he was not alive. The publican
who beat his breast and confessed his sins in anguish, he was
alive. The younger brother—the one we have all been—was
dead when he was drinking and whoring away his patrimony,
but when he felt the pain of hunger and the sharper pinch of
guilt, he came to life again, repented, and returned home. The
elder brother, who felt no joy at hearing that the sinner had
come home, wavered between death and life, and we do not
know whether he opened his heart at last.

Jesus called His suffering a "cup"; we must remember that
cups are for tasting and for drinking down. Jesus, says a friend of
mine, *tasted* death. He drank it to the lees. One of the bystand-
ers wished to give him a sponge soaked in gall, an anodyne that
would ease the living fire of His torn and exposed nerves. Jesus
refused it.

He did not die resigned. He was not Socrates, waiting to be
given the hemlock, bidding farewell to his wife and children,

and conversing with his friends. He was not Cardinal Wolsey, deposed from his position as chancellor of England, who lay on his deathbed musing upon an ill-spent career, saying that if he had served God half so well as he had served his king, Henry VIII, God would not have thus left him to his enemies. He was not the Stoic philosopher Seneca, bleeding to death by his own hand, having been notified by his former pupil, the emperor Nero, that his life was no longer desired. The mysterious cry from the cross, "My God, my God, why hast thou forsaken me?" (Matt. 27:46) is the cry of a man who is utterly devoted, who loves His people to the end, who does nothing but what He sees the Father do. In His very dereliction He calls upon the name of the Lord, in an agony of love.

In all of recorded history and in all of the tales of heroes, there is no death like the death of Jesus, not one. If the Gospel writers wished to make something up, they would have done what even the best writers do. They would have turned to models. They might have looked to the noble Hector, having suffered a mortal wound in the throat, begging his slayer Achilles to return his body to his people. They might have looked to the great king David, who spent his last hour advising his son Solomon to follow the way of the Lord, and to make sure that his old general Joab did not go down to the grave in peace. Not even in the histories of the Christian martyrs, who sometimes seem to have had a Roman or Greek flair about them—"Turn me over," said Saint Lawrence as they roasted his flesh on the gridiron, "I'm done on this side"—do we find this unimaginable combination of utter love, utter embrace of sorrow, and utter submission to the will of the Father. No one preached as Jesus did. No one died as Jesus did. And no one rose from the dead—which Jesus did.

My God, My God

I remember the day my father died. He was sitting in his chair in the living room. The television was on, although I'm not sure he was watching it. Occasionally he drifted into a mild sleep, but most of the time he was alert. He knew that he was going to die that day, because he had no longer been able to swallow any water, and his kidneys had begun to fail. My brother, my sisters, and I had come home to be with him and our mother. We were nervous. We talked in that stupid distracted way that people have when they don't know what else to do. One time my father even asked us to quiet down. He could hardly speak. I don't know if he felt lonely. I don't know if he felt grateful for our presence. He had had the last rites. Now he was waiting.

He could have asked to be admitted to a hospital, to be fed water and sugar through a tube, but he saw no point in it. He wanted to be home. When at last his breathing became labored, we surrounded him, touching him, calling his name. He looked toward my mother with his eyes wide open. He whispered into her ear, "I love you," and then he was gone.

How strange a thing it is to say. His body was still there. We shut the eyes and called the funeral director, who came promptly and took the body away. But *he* was not there. The soul had departed. That separation, I think, is the empty core of death.

God warned Adam and Eve not to eat of the forbidden fruit, because on the day they did so, they would die. We suppose that God mercifully deferred the punishment to a later day, since Adam and Eve lived for a long time thereafter and had many children. But the separation, that essential emptiness, came at once. They hid from the Lord God. They were ashamed of their nakedness before one another. Adam blamed Eve, and Eve blamed the serpent. They were alienated from the world; Adam would have to earn his bread by the sweat of his brow, and Eve would bring forth children in pain. Their son Cain, looking with envy upon the sacrifice of his brother Abel, would slay him and would retort, when God confronted him, "Am I my brother's keeper?" (Gen. 4:9). And thus, the sacred author has concentrated the whole history of the world into a few short pages. It is a history of separation, husband from wife, brother from brother, man from the world, and man from God.

So if the Lord were to assume our human nature and suffer, while sinless, all the consequences of sin, He would have to enter into our separation, our having cast ourselves out into the wilderness, even our feeling abandoned by God. I am not making light of the cruelty of His physical suffering. The lashes laid bare His spinal cord. He was half-dead from loss of blood before they yoked the Cross to His neck. To take the merest breath He had to lift Himself up on the cross by flexing His knees inward, putting pressure on His feet, which were nailed to a slanted brace that would provide just enough leverage to keep the miserable convicts alive, extending their torment. His heart raced to provide a little oxygen to the blood. He went into congestive heart failure, His lungs filling with the water that John saw flowing from His pierced side.

But that physical suffering, as terrible as it was, was little enough compared with the experience of separation. A hardened criminal might snarl a bit to learn that his fellow conspirator had betrayed him. But he would not feel the yawning depth of disappointment; of loss of friendship; he would not miss the evil brother. Yet what did Jesus see, when He looked down from the Cross? A few women, who were not afraid of the Romans, possibly because the Romans would not trouble themselves with them, and the young apostle John. Peter, the Rock, was like sand sifting through the fingers. He had denied knowing Jesus, so that he could spy about the praetorium, and then he had fled. So had the rest. There were some Jews below, chief representatives of the chosen people to whom the Father had revealed the law and the coming of the Messiah. They seem to have felt some smug curiosity. They mocked Him, telling Him that if He was the Son of God, He should come down from the Cross, not understanding that He would die upon that Cross precisely because He was the Son of God. And when He cried out, no doubt with nearly suffocated breath, they misunderstood Him, and thought He was calling upon the prophet Elijah.

It is a mystery I cannot pretend to penetrate. It is a deeper mystery than the creation of the world from nothing. For here we have God Himself reduced to nothing; God severed from man, and even from God. *Eloi, eloi, lama sabacthani?* cried the Lord. "My God, my God, why hast thou forsaken me?" In the bleakest night of our lives these words shine bright, because they shed their stark light upon the heart of human agony — the death in death, the loneliness, the fling of the heart to the beloved, when we cannot see that the beloved is there. Only a man could utter these words, yet no man would have invented them for Jesus to utter. We can rest assured that they are as true and as solid as rock. Many a Christian will die with the consolations of the Church beside him; the priest to anoint his brow, the wayfarer's food to sustain him for the last leg of the journey; loved ones to pray with him, even to sing with him. Those are the mercies of God. But Christ denied Himself that mercy.

"Yea," says the psalmist, "though I walk through the valley of the shadow of death, I will fear no evil: for thou art with me" (Ps. 23:4). That is true; God does not abandon us. But we do not always feel the truth. There are times when the shadow of death feels like an impenetrable darkness. At those times, we should remember that wherever we go, Jesus has been there before us and that there is no depth of sorrow or anguish, no power of evil and no principality of death, that can separate us from the love of God that we find in Him and through Him.

And that fidelity is evident even in the words of Jesus' cry. We could well note that the psalm begins with those words, but does not end with them. It is the psalm that the Church sees as a prophecy of the sufferings of Jesus upon the Cross:

> I am a worm, and no man, a reproach of men, and
>   despised by the people.
> All they that see me laugh me to scorn: they shoot
>   out the lip, they shake the head, saying,
> "He trusted in the Lord, that He would deliver him.
> Let Him deliver him, seeing that He delighted in
>   him." . . .
> For dogs have compassed me: the assembly of the
>   wicked have enclosed me: they pierced my hands
>   and my feet.
> I can count all my bones; they look upon me and
>   stare at me.
> They part my garments among them, and for my
>   vesture they cast lots. (Ps. 22:6-8, 16-18)

But the psalmist turns this agony into triumph, proclaiming in the end that God has heard the cry of His afflicted one. And perhaps we hear the ring of hope in Jesus' words. He addresses the Father as *Eloi*, "my God." It is not the Hebrew of the psalm that He is uttering, but rather the dialect of Aramaic, the intimate language of His family and His neighbors. Jesus has cast the words of the psalm into that tongue. It is as if He were pouring out all His being into the cry. Jesus never looks upon God as a mere force, something distant and abstract, but always as the Father, because that is who God is. And His oneness with the Father, even in this moment of darkness, is expressed in that simple vowel at the end of the word for God. Not *El, El* does He cry, but *Eloi, Eloi:* my God, my God.

Each one of us will come to the moment of passage. Jesus has been there. He leads us, He suffers beside us, He strengthens us, and if it seems sometimes that all is lost, Jesus has known that time too, and will guide us through that shadow. For it is a shadow, a kind of nothing. Beyond that shadow there is Someone, and His name is Love.

Chapter 17

He Is Risen Indeed

Some ten years before, much to his own surprise, he entered the Catholic Church, the essayist Malcolm Muggeridge was finding his way back to Jesus. Muggeridge had seen the emptiness of what the twentieth century had to offer to mankind. Sex devoid of meaning, the accumulation of creature comforts, the evil buffoonery of Nazism, the more efficient evil of communism, the dehumanizing effects of socialism generally—he had seen it, even believed in some of it at one time, and now rejected it with a hearty laugh. To whom would he turn then, if not to Jesus? The words of Saint Peter rang in his heart: "Lord, to whom shall we go? Thou hast the words of eternal life" (John 6:68).

So Muggeridge said, and again this is *before* his conversion:

I believe that Jesus Christ is alive now, that, as it were, his life is still valid, so that it is possible, not only to hear and learn, but *experience*, the truths that he propounded.... I know absolutely, without any question, that you can derive strength and illumination from a relationship with the man in the Gospels which you cannot achieve, we'll say for instance with Socrates, who was a very wise and good man who also died.

Reflections on the Christian Life

That is a remarkable fact. Muslims do not have a relationship with Mohammed. They might consider such a thing to be blasphemous. Buddhists do not have a relationship with the Buddha. They learn from him, they follow his example, they honor his enlightenment, but they do not devote themselves to him. Even Jews do not claim a personal relationship with Moses. People who study ancient philosophy do not claim to bring Socrates into their hearts. Socrates was but a man, and all men die. When we consider the great movers and shakers of the world, a Pericles or a Bismarck or a Michelangelo, whether they were good men or bad, they seem no more than cardboard figures in a historical diorama for a museum, compared with Jesus. And that is exactly what Jesus Himself said: "Heaven and earth shall pass away, but my words shall not pass away" (Matt. 24:35).

In the previous chapter, I set myself the impossible task to meditate upon the death of Jesus, a death like no other in recorded history; and we Christians believe that there could never be a death like His, because He was the Son of God made flesh. But I have seen people die. I have never seen anyone rise from the dead. "People who are dead don't rise to life again!" an unbeliever once protested to my pastor. "I do believe," he replied, "that *that was the point*."

How can I write about You, my risen Lord? What do I know about victory over the grave?

I might muse upon a few astonishing correlations. What is the most fascinating artifact from the ancient world—one that defies explanation, with nothing even closely resembling it? The Shroud of Turin. How strange, that it should be associated with an event that is also absolutely singular, the Resurrection of Jesus! What are the most unusual and unprepared-for books in antiquity? There were poems, there were chronicles, there were oratorical declamations, there were philosophical dialogues, there were beast fables and myths about the sexual habits of the gods, but before Matthew, Mark, Luke, and John, there was *nothing* like the Gospels. It is absolutely a new form of writing, presenting to us the most powerful character in the history of literature, and these are not professional writers — in fact, at least three of them, Matthew, Mark, and John, do not speak Greek as their first tongue. How strange is it, that this new literary form should arise in connection with that singular event, the Resurrection of Jesus!

And then there is the stunning spread of the Church to all the corners of the world. It has fulfilled the ancient promise God made to Abraham, that his descendants should be as numerous as the grains of sand on the shore, or the stars in the heavens. It has fulfilled the commission Jesus gave to His disciples after His Resurrection: "Go ye therefore, and teach all nations, baptizing them in the name of the Father, and of the Son, and of the Holy Ghost" (Matt. 28:19). It is an event of colossal significance. Nothing else matches it. Nothing comes close. How strange, that it should spring from that singular event, the thing that happened on that morning after the Sabbath, long ago!

I say that there never has been an event like it. But perhaps there was one. When God said, "Let there be light," He made a world of intelligibility and beauty and goodness. The world was made from nothing, by God's good will; and that means that God could never be reduced to the world, or drowned in history, so to speak. God reveals Himself to us as one who stands outside of all history, transcending the material world. But God also beheld what He made and saw that it was very good. So He is no deist god in unapproachable solitude, indifferent to the world and to mankind in it. The attitude of the pious Jew or Christian can never be that the world is something to be shuffled off, escaped. The world is real, and good. God works in that world. He is the guide of human history.

The meaning of the whole course of history, and the meaning of the story of any human being's life, is to be found in those two events, the creation of the world and the redemption of the world. They are things that happened, one at the beginning of time, the other at the fulcrum of time. But they point beyond time. The fulfillment of human desire cannot be found in time, but every blessing that we receive in time springs from the fount of all grace, the God who made the world, the God who redeemed the world, and the God who dwells in the hearts of all believers, bringing the redeemed world to its consummation at the end of time.

All this may sound abstract. It is not. It is more real than the earth beneath my feet. It is infinitely more real than the dreams of power that technology offers us. It is the life of life.

When you meet the true Christian, you find that he does not talk about religion. He may not even be particularly interested in religion as such. He talks about Jesus. For what shall we say about religion? The ancient Carthaginians worshiped a fertility god, Moloch, whom the poet Milton described most aptly:

> First Moloch, horrid king with blood besmear'd
> Of human sacrifice, and parents' tears,
> Though for the noise of drums and timbrels loud
> Their children's cries unheard, that pass'd through fire
> To his grim Idol. (*Paradise Lost*, Bk. 1)

The Carthaginians would set a child in the arms of the idol, arms that were pitched slightly downward, so that after a few moments it would fall into the consuming flames below. A large necropolis has been excavated near the ruined city, filled with little bones. In the western world we have resumed the worship of this despicable idol. That too is religion, just as the horrible experiments of the Nazi doctor Josef Mengele were science, and as, in a way, the imbecilic obscenities of *Lady Chatterley's Lover* are literature. Some people, disdaining the word *religious*, describe themselves as "spiritual," forgetting that Satan is a spiritual being, and that the worst of evils, pride and envy, are spiritual. But let us clear these foul things from our minds. The true Christian is the one who looks to Jesus, who searches for the face of Jesus, who finds Jesus in his fellowmen, who hears the words of Jesus and follows them, and who cannot contemplate Jesus without wishing to break out in the exclamation of the apostle Thomas, "My Lord and my God!" (John 20:28).

Now, people do not talk that way about Socrates or Confucius. They talk that way about Jesus, because He is risen. Note the tense of the verb. We do not simply say, "Jesus rose from the dead." Yes, He did, but we mean more. We mean that death has no more dominion over Him. He died once and dies no more. He *is risen:* His Resurrection from the dead is not an event that happened and is past, but is the defining event for all mankind, now and forever. Even if mankind were to discover some way to prolong our bodily functions indefinitely, sentencing billions of people to the terrible banality of living only to keep living, that would be but a clumsy caricature of the newness of life, eternal life, that Jesus offers. It would be like the drone of a machine, compared with a symphony of joy.

Recently there was a soccer match at a stadium in Russia, scheduled on Easter. All at once, the crowd on one side cried out, "Christ is risen!" And the thousands on the other side replied, "He is risen indeed!" It was as if eighty years of communism, with its official atheism and its hatred of the Lord, had vanished, like the traces of a nightmare, when you wake up and see the sunlight flooding into the room. Who would have thought, when the Soviet Union was at its peak of military power, that the empire would crumble so quickly—and that the common people, decades later, would be echoing the ancient words of joy, just as they always had? Christ is risen indeed!

What is happening to Russia, what is happening in the scorched lands of eastern Europe, what is happening among the pariahs of India, and the hopeless businessmen of the far East, is the story of the Resurrection of Jesus. People may rebel, they may try to repress it, but they cannot escape it. And some embrace it. Some will say, with Saint Paul, that they no longer live, but that Christ lives in them (cf. Gal. 2:20).

When we meet someone who says, "No longer I, but Christ in me," we are like Mary and the other holy women, on that bright morning. We become witnesses to a rising from the dead. I've visited a maximum-security prison, to meet and speak with a group of lay Dominican brothers, most of them serving life sentences. I've mentioned one of them already. The men sang out gloriously at Mass. One said to me, "Prison is the best thing that ever happened in my life, because it gave me freedom, by taking away my choices." In his eyes I saw shining what Saint Paul calls "the glorious liberty of the children of God" (Rom. 8:21). His life had been transformed. He was a friend of the risen Lord. There is a pastor of a Baptist church a mile from my house. He too spent years in prison, for rape. There he too met Jesus. Now he is a witness to the transforming power of the Resurrection.

He Is Risen Indeed

In every person we meet, if we keep our eyes and hearts open, we can see Jesus. The Lord so commands us. "Whatever you do," He says, "to the least of these, you do unto me." He does not say, "It is as if you did it unto me," but rather He identifies Himself with every single human being who crosses our path.

Some people are poor because they are poor; others are poor because they are rich; some are fools because they are slow of wit, and others are fools because they are quick and shallow. We are not a glorious lot! But everyone is Jesus to us. And that means, too, that in everyone there is a vision of the risen Lord. It may be that the next person you meet will come forth from the valley of the shadow of death, because you obeyed the Lord and ministered to him, and he saw Jesus in your face. It may also be that the next person you meet will present to you the face of Jesus, because you yourself are in dire need, in poverty of means or wisdom or love.

And this will often happen when we least expect it. Muggeridge recalls a time when he and a friend were filming a show on the Holy Land. Again, this was before he submitted himself to the Faith. He affirmed that whatever happens to our civilization—even if we cast our lot with a Herod or a Pontius Pilate or a Caiaphas and are therefore forgotten to the world—the light of Christ will continue to shine in our darkness. But it did not remain abstract with him, not even then. He and his friend went for a walk along the road to Emmaus, and as they walked along, recalling the events of the Crucifixion, and considering its meaning for our own world, they felt they were joined by another, a third man. Muggeridge thus concludes a sermon he delivered at Saint Giles in Edinburgh: "And I tell you that wherever the walk, and whoever the wayfarers, there is always this third presence ready to emerge from the shadows and fall in step along the dusty, stony way."

He is right about that. But, as he well knew, the story did not end on the Emmaus road. It came to its fulfillment in the wayside inn. "Abide with us," the disciples said to Jesus (Luke 24:29), not knowing who it was who had been speaking with them that afternoon and explaining the Scriptures to them. He did, and when they were at the table, He took the bread, said the blessing, and broke it. And then they knew Him, and He vanished from their sight.

Jesus is with us on our journey. But He is the risen Lord, who Himself provides the food for the journey. And the journey's end is not some endless life such as we know it now. The story does not simply go on and on. A story that has no goal is not a story at all, but just a string of episodes, with no ultimate meaning. The journey to Emmaus, accompanied by Jesus, ends with the Eucharist, and partaking of the feast of the risen Christ. "Behold," says the One seated upon the throne, at the wedding feast of the Lamb, "I make all things new" (Rev. 21:5).

Years later, Muggeridge entered that Church, and received the Body of Christ, risen and never to die again. So, wayfaring Christian, if someone asks you where you are going, reply, "I am going to a feast, and so is the rest of the Church. Where else should we go? It's the morning of Easter."

Christ is risen. He is risen indeed, *alleluia*!

Chapter 18

The End of the Story,
Which Is the Beginning

And on the seventh day God ended his work which he had made; and he rested on the seventh day from all his work which he had made. And God blessed the seventh day, and sanctified it: because that in it he had rested from all his work which God created and made. (Gen. 2:2-3)

A group of boys gather round their acknowledged leader, a young man who had been a monk, but who was now going forth into the world to witness to the love of Christ. They had not always been faithful and generous, these boys. In fact, they had subjected one among them, Ilyusha — the son of a poor pathetic man and a half-mad woman — to mockery and scorn. But the young monk, Alyosha, had taken Ilyusha's part, and had won the rest of the boys over, not only to natural kindness, but to that charity which Christ alone can give. And now they are gathered together to attend the breakfast for Ilyusha's funeral.

Alyosha understands that this moment is not simply an instant of time like any other, as if time were a river beginning in nothing and nowhere and ending in nothing and nowhere. It is a moment whose significance transcends time. So he speaks to the boys. He begs them to recall this morning, and their fellowship together, years later, when perhaps some of them will have wandered far from what is true and good; and he assures them that even the memory of it will bring grace to them.

Then the boys ask him the question of questions, the one that sees the meaning of time in eternity. "Will we see one another again in heaven?" they ask. "Will we know one another?" And Alyosha replies with laughter, "Assuredly we will see and know one another!" To which the boys cheer, "Hurrah for Karamazov!"

Those are the last words to Fyodor Dostoyevsky's novel *The Brothers Karamazov.* I had almost written *the final words,* but that would not be quite right. They are not final at all, in the sense of something over and done with. They are, it is true, the words to which all the events of the novel are leading, their end and goal, but it is an end that is not an end but a beginning. It is an exclamation of joy and communion in Christ. It is a peal of praise. It is not wholly bound to the events of that morning in the Russian village, just as the power of the story is not bound to the age in which Dostoyevsky wrote. No matter who I may be or where I am—a soldier preparing for war in the Pacific, the father of a family in his comfortable home, a scientist delving into the mystery of that impossible substance known as water, two hundred years from now—the story is for me, and I am invited to join that cheer.

So it seems to me that all stories, and all works of genuine art, point beyond themselves; they put their roots down into time and place, but their fruit has the savor of eternity. Consider for example Michelangelo's *David.* It was commissioned to commemorate the victory by the Florentines over their perennial rival, Pisa. But if someone were to say that that is what the sculpture means, that that is all it is, we would look upon him as if a blind man were to instruct us about the rainbow. The temporal, political, and economic occasion of a thing is not the thing itself. If someone else were to say, "This is a sculpture of a nude young man, done with considerable anatomical accuracy, evidence of tremendous technical skill," we would agree, just as we would accept the historian's word about Florence and Pisa. But still such a comment would miss the soul of the master-piece. It would reduce the work of art to a description of the material thing represented, without regard to the meaning. It would miss the intense glare in David's eyes, bespeaking a spiri-tual zeal far beyond anything achieved or even understood by the great sculptors of ancient Greece. It would miss that strik-ing combination of physical beauty and ruggedness, of poise and suffering, that characterizes the youth's large hands, their knuckles swollen with the calluses of hard work. It would miss the meaning of the very *being* of the youth who said, "Who is this uncircumcised Philistine, that he should defy the armies of the living God?" (1 Sam. 17:26).

Someone may say, "Stories are only fictions. They are what we impose upon events that in themselves have no meaning." There are two responses to such a claim. First, it is impossible to live by that unbelief. Even atheists have their stories, and outlandish ones at that. They too spin yarns, tired old things about the inevitable advancement of technology that will bring us all truces among nations and psychological contentment and bin-fattened-turkey dinners with cranberry sauce and sweaty pornography on the television, as we climb onward and upward toward making ourselves into gods. If you do not believe that our lives are essentially stories, do not contradict yourself by talking to me nonsense about progress.

Second, we do not regard ourselves as imposing meaning on the meaningless—an imposition that would be arbitrary and self-contradictory. We regard ourselves as searching for meaning that is already there to be found. The scientist who looks for order will often find it where it is least to be expected. For example, if it were not for the gigantic mass of the planet Jupiter, the earth's orbit would be unstable, and the earth itself would be bombarded with cosmic buckshot—which Jupiter swallows up like a big vacuum cleaner. Vivaldi incorporated the sweetness of bird song into his *Four Seasons*; the beauty and the order were given to him, and he accepted them and wove them into his art. William Blake encouraged us to see the world in a grain of sand, and the heavens in a wildflower. It is not an act of pretending, in pride, but of beholding, in gratitude.

I should like to say that the story that directs us to the truth is precisely the story that leads us to the threshold of transcendence: it is the story that brings us always to the dawn. Not all stories do that. The story above, of man's ever-increasing domination of nature, if it is the only story we know, brings us to an interminable evening of full bellies and boredom. The old Norse sagas, immeasurably nobler than the myths of technology, ended with mankind and the gods of light battling against the giants and the gods of darkness, wherein those Germanic warriors would show their bravery, ever more admirable in defeat than in victory. But the gods of darkness would triumph, and the world would return to its original chaos—the story ending in arctic winter without a spring.

In his *Theogony*—the title means "Birth of the Gods"— Hesiod recounts how one generation of gods was replaced by another, until finally Zeus, through brute force combined with cunning political alliances, dethroned his father, Cronus, and became, by virtue of his power and *not* his original paternity, "the father of men and gods." It is essentially a story that ends with the Greek city-state. There is nothing in Hesiod past that condition.

What an infinite abyss separates the account in Genesis from all of these! There we learn that there is nothing beyond creation but God. From God does it take its origin, and in God does it find its meaning; He is the one who gives all creatures their being, and who blesses them, and commands them to be fruitful and to multiply. But the six days of creation all point toward the seventh day of Sabbath rest. In other words, the "end" of the story of creation is the very rest, the unending joy of God, who never ceases to rest in action, and never ceases to act in rest. The creation story does not point to some political or economic state, or to the doom of darkness, like a universal heat-death, Viking style. It points instead to abundant life. It is what the prophets and the psalmists mean when they talk about the joy of going up to the house of the Lord. People do not derive joy from mere ritual. The joy of the rite springs from its orientation toward a beauty that always surpasses what we now can behold. It is the joy of the Sabbath, not considered as one day among seven, but as the fulfillment and the meaning of all days. It is a joy that is inseparable from our acknowledging that we have been *created*, and that therefore we do not make our own meaning, nor do we look for our fulfillment in what we can bring about by our unaided work in time:

> *Make a joyful noise unto the Lord, all ye lands.*
> *Serve the Lord with gladness: come before his*
> *presence with singing.*
> *Know ye that the Lord he is God: it is he that*
> *hath made us, and not we ourselves; we are*
> *his people, and the sheep of his pasture.*

Reflections on the Christian Life

Enter into his gates with thanksgiving, and into
his courts with praise: be thankful unto him,
and bless his name.
For the Lord is good; his mercy is everlasting; and
his truth endureth to all generations. (Ps. 100)

In the last century, we in the West have fallen into the lazy habit of reducing things to such component parts as we can see and manipulate. So we say that a star is "only" a cloud of hydrogen fusing into helium and giving off intense energy. I call this the constitutional fallacy. It does injustice to the splendor of the star's being, and it is downright absurd when we apply it to a person. We would be compelled by it to say that, for example, the life of Saint Peter was but a series of momentary physical events, one after another, with no more coherence than that of a drift of sand in the desert wind. But everything in our experience directs us the other way. We come to know a person, not a bag of biological odds and ends, and a person has a life. It is true that the meaning of that life cannot simply be one of those things that the life contains, one element among others in the story. It is instead something intimated by the whole. That apostle who blurted out, atop the mountain of transfiguration, "Master, it is good for us to be here" (Mark 9:5), the same impulsive fisherman who stepped out of the boat to try to walk toward Jesus on the water, the one who at first refused to allow Jesus to wash his feet—he was the one who would be crucified in Rome, upside down, the first head of the Church to die witnessing to Jesus. From the saint that he became—from something within the story of his life but beyond it, just as grace springs from a well beyond the world—do we understand all that he had been, including the fellow who hauled ashore the net bursting with fish, and spoke those words steeped in sadness and truth, "Depart from me; for I am a sinful man, O Lord" (Luke 5:8).

What I am trying to say—and what many have said before me, more clearly and eloquently—is that because we are persons, and because our lives are indeed stories, our end cannot be here, and the meaning of our lives must lie beyond. This truth is presented to us from the first words of Genesis, "In the beginning God created the heavens and the earth," to the last words of Revelation, "The grace of our Lord Jesus Christ be with you all. Amen."

And it appears to us in an astonishing way in the last events of the life of Jesus in the flesh on earth. The Apostles themselves spent the rest of their lives meditating upon it; they could not have come up with it on their own. We, who have inherited it and two thousand years of reflection on its meaning, still can hardly understand it.

Let us recall their errors. They believed that the Messiah would come to establish a just kingdom on earth, and that all nations would come to Jerusalem to worship. And that has in fact happened, but not at all as they expected it. For their hopes were too timid. The story would have been closed, so to speak, in an earthly institution. Granted, that institution they anticipated, the Temple victorious, would have directed the hearts of men to the living God, and the joy of the Sabbath would have been showered upon the earth like spring rain. But that would be the end. It would be the most glorious version imaginable of the error that locates the meaning of the human story *within* human history, here at the earthly end brought about by God.

Then, when they saw Jesus, some of them thought He was a ghost. If that was what He was, what follows? Perhaps our lives end in some insubstantial, shadowy existence, such as the specters in Homer's *Odyssey* endured—an existence that made the proud Achilles say that he would prefer to be the meanest plowhand upon the sunlit earth rather than king among all the sightless dead. Or perhaps we leave the material world utterly behind, ascending to a "pure" realm of spirit. In either case, the story of our lives would end in unmeaning.

But Jesus proved to them that His body was true. He ate with them. He directed the hand of Thomas to probe the wound in His side. But what if they then came to suppose that Jesus would remain with them on earth? What if He had merely come back to life such as we know it? What if He had been revivified, like Lazarus or like Jairus's child? Then we would be thrust back upon our original question: What does this life of ours mean? The story would continue, but we could make no sense of it, not having the eternal vantage from which to read it.

Let us return to that Easter morning. It was the day *after* the Sabbath when the women went to the tomb to anoint Jesus' body. They could not do so on Friday, because Jesus had died in the late afternoon; there had been no time. They could not do so on the Sabbath, which began on Friday at sundown; it was against the law of Moses to do any work on the Sabbath, much less to be defiled by contact with a dead body. They waited, then, until the morning of the day after the Sabbath. They came to the tomb on the *eighth day*. Saint Peter, meditating upon the significance of the number, and on the mysterious time between Christ's death and Resurrection, compares Baptism in the Church to Noah's ark, wherein eight souls were saved—Noah and his wife and their three sons and their wives, saved for a new world. Saint Augustine drew the conclusion that if the seventh day is the day of the eternal Sabbath, it is also the eighth day, a day that has a morning but no evening, the day of resurrection. For every day in the creation of the world, the sacred author says that there was an evening and a morning, except for the seventh day, the day of consummation. But that seventh day without an evening brings to the world what the world could not imagine: the dawn of the eighth day, the "bright morning star" that is the Lord (Rev. 22:16).

If we are to see in every one of our neighbors the face of Christ, we must understand that the meaning of his life, and of our own, streams forth from Christ, who is the Alpha and Omega, the first and the last. That more than sums up our stories. If we accept the grace of God, if we join our hearts with Jesus, if we allow the Spirit to dwell within us, we and all that we have seen and loved and endured and done will be among those things made new by the One seated upon the throne. So wrote C. S. Lewis of the children of Narnia, who had entered Paradise: "All their life in this world and all their adventures in Narnia had only been the cover and the title page: now at last they were beginning Chapter One of the Great Story which no one on earth has read: which goes on forever: in which every chapter is better than the one before."

The meaning of our lives? Here it is:

> In the beginning was the Word, and the Word
>   was with God, and the Word was God.
> The same was in the beginning with God.
> All things were made in him; and without him
>   was not any thing made that was made.
> In him was life, and the life was the light of men.
> And the light shineth in darkness, and the darkness
>   comprehended it not.

Reflections on the Christian Life

*There was a man sent from God, whose
name was John.
The same came for a witness, to bear witness
of the Light, that all men through him might
believe.
He was not that Light, but was sent to bear
witness of that Light.
That was the true Light, which lighteth every
man that cometh into the world.
He was in the world, and the world was made
by him, and the world knew him not.
He came into his own, and his own received
him not.
But as many as received him, to them gave he
power to become the sons of God, even to
them that believe on his name:
Which were born, not of blood, nor of the will of
the flesh, nor of the will of man, but of God.
And the Word was made flesh, and dwelt among us,
(and we beheld his glory, the glory as of the only
begotten of the Father) full of grace and truth.
John bare witness of him, and cried, saying, This
was he of whom I spake, He that cometh after
me is preferred before me: for he was before me.
And of his fullness have all we received, and
grace for grace.
For the law was given by Moses, but grace and
truth came by Jesus Christ.
No man hath seen God at any time; the only
begotten Son, which is in the bosom of the
Father, he hath declared him. (John 1:1-18)*

Anthony Esolen

Anthony Esolen is professor of English at Providence College. He is the author or translator of twelve books, including a three-volume translation of Dante's *Divine Comedy*; *Ironies of Faith: The Laughter at the Heart of Christian Literature*; and *The Beauty of the Word*, a running commentary on the new English translation of the Mass. He writes regularly for *Touchstone, Crisis, Public Discourse, Catholic World Report, First Things,* and *Magnificat.* He and his wife, Debra, and their children, Jessica and David, live in Rhode Island.

An Invitation

Reader, the book that you hold in your hands was published by Sophia Institute Press.

Sophia Institute seeks to restore man's knowledge of eternal truth, including man's knowledge of his own nature, his relation to other persons, and his relation to God.

Our press fulfills this mission by offering translations, reprints, and new publications. We offer scholarly as well as popular publications; there are works of fiction along with books that draw from all the arts and sciences of our civilization. These books afford readers a rich source of the enduring wisdom of mankind.

Sophia Institute Press is the publishing arm of the Thomas More College of Liberal Arts and Holy Spirit College. Both colleges are dedicated to providing university-level education in the Western tradition under the guiding light of Catholic teaching.

If you know a young person who might be interested in the ideas found in this book, share it. If you know a young person seeking a college that takes seriously the adventure of learning and the quest for truth, bring our institutions to his attention.

www.SophiaInstitute.com
www.ThomasMoreCollege.edu
www.HolySpiritCollege.org

SOPHIA INSTITUTE PRESS

THE PUBLISHING DIVISION OF